D0509967

THE APPLE BOOK

THE
APPLE
BOOK

Jane Simpson
and Gill MacLennan

Illustrated by Cherry Denman

THE BODLEY HEAD

LONDON SYDNEY

TORONTO

HIGHLAND
LIBRARIES

HIGHLAND
REGIONAL
LIBRARY

50 14890

WITHDRAWN
641.6411

British Library Cataloguing
in Publication Data
Simpson, Jane, 1944–
The apple book
1. Cookery (Apples)
I. Title   II. MacLennan, Gill
641.6'411   TX813.A6
ISBN 0 370 30617 1

© Jane Simpson and Gill MacLennan 1984
Printed in Great Britain for
The Bodley Head Ltd
9 Bow Street, London WC2E 7AL
by William Clowes, Beccles
First published 1984

CONTENTS

AUTHORS' FOREWORDS

I would never have thought of writing a book on cooking with apples had we not moved to a house with an old tangled orchard at the bottom of the garden. The first year we watched with excitement as our trees became covered with a cloud of pale pink blossom, followed by a mass of tiny apples. But as the apples grew our eagerness turned to alarm. What could we do with thousands of apples?

We began by making cider, sharing a huge old-fashioned press with a friend nearby. It was a great success and we have made cider ever since. But we still had a mass of fruit. Fond as I am of apple puddings the recipes I knew were in danger of becoming monotonous. I improvised, sometimes wildly, and some of the best results came about by chance experiments.

It was during one of those apple-filled autumns that Gill came to stay. She had just come down from the Highlands to work as a cookery writer on a magazine and it was a real treat to have another cook in the house. Though we had many tastes in common we were drawn to different styles of cooking, Gill to the spicy pungent flavours of the East and I to the more delicate creamy food of Normandy. Between us, we could produce not just the cookery book that I would dearly have loved that first apple-filled year, but one which would appeal to everyone.

I would like to thank Gill for catching my enthusiasm, Jonathan and Maria Brunskill for introducing me to The Bodley Head, Kit Trimble for allowing us to treat his garden as a cider house, Chris Archer for allowing us to illustrate his home-made cider press, Mrs Shepherd of the

East Malling Research Station for her advice on apples in general, and finally my family for being such willing and honest guinea pigs.

Jane Simpson

When I first moved to London, a quiet country lass from the Highlands, I had, like so many others who arrive in search of fame and fortune, nowhere to live.

My grandmother came to the rescue. A friend of hers had relatives in London, and as the man of the house was a journalist, she reasoned it would be a good idea to look them up if I was seriously going to launch myself into the world of publishing.

And so I met the Simpson family. Instead of the streets of London paved with gold, I found the Surrey countryside littered with apples, and was caught up in the family enthusiasm for the apple harvest, culminating in the cider-making weekend. As we collapsed in front of the fire at the end of the day, with a contented sigh and a glass of last year's vintage, we wondered what other people did with all their apples — those who weren't lucky enough to have a part share in a cider press, those people with even *one* tree in the garden. Wouldn't it be lovely to be able to pick up a single book jammed full of good apple recipes, instead of having to leaf through lots of books for inspiration?

And so the idea of *The Apple Book* was born.

My thanks to my grandmother for introducing me to the unsuspecting Simpson family; to Colin, Jane, Millie and Matthew for their kindness when I first moved south of the border; to my friend Liz for her speedy and accurate typing; and finally to my flatmates in London for their enthusiasm and considered criticism. Anything I cook now is greeted with amused suspicion and the inevitable question — is there apple in it? Sometimes it's hard to tell.

Gill MacLennan

THE
APPLE
HARVEST

Apples on the same tree ripen over a period of time; the ones on the outside of the tree ripen first as they are nearest the sunlight. The easiest way to tell if an apple is ready to be picked is to place it in the palm of the hand and gently twist it. If it comes away from the tree easily with its stalk intact it is ready for picking.

You may find that you have a huge crop of apples one year and hardly any the next. Some varieties are more inclined to crop biennially than others, but you can help your trees to fruit every year. If you thin out the clusters in mid-summer, when the trees naturally shed some of their surplus fruit, you will prevent the trees over-cropping and get bigger and better fruit each time. Thin out the clusters leaving a 4 in (10 cm) gap between apples. Large cooking apples can be even more widely spaced.

PICKING AND STORING

It is a simple fact that some apples store better than others. Early ripening apples should be eaten as soon as possible after they are picked, mid-season varieties cannot be kept for more than a few weeks. Late varieties are the ones to store. They will taste delicious if they are left to ripen on the tree but if they are to be stored for the winter they should be picked before they are ripe, and ripened in store.

Apples to be stored must be in perfect condition. Pick the apples carefully and gently place them in a smooth-sided receptacle. A bucket is better than a wicker basket which can tear the apple's delicate skin. Leave them to cool off overnight in the open or in a cool, airy room, then check them over thoroughly and discard any that are even slightly damaged or have no stalk. Store in a cool, dark place, ideally at a steady temperature of 40°F (3.5°C) and well away from potatoes, pears or anything with a strong smell like paint, creosote or onions.

There are basically two ways of packing apples. Whichever way you choose check them often and thoroughly and remove any suspect fruit, as a rotten apple is as infectious as a child with measles!

You can wrap them in ordinary thin polythene food bags which prevent the apples from drying out and becoming shrivelled if they are stored somewhere with less than adequate ventilation such as an attic. As a little air should be allowed to circulate, seal the mouth of the bag and make two pin pricks in different parts of the bag for each 2 lb (900 g) of apples but take care not to puncture the skins.

Alternatively store the apples in seed trays stacked on top of each other or packed in the moulded card or polystyrene trays used by commercial packers which greengrocers are usually happy to give away. The apples must not touch each other, so slip a largish screw of newspaper between them or wrap them in specially made oiled wraps which are available from most garden centres. Oiled wraps help keep fruit in good condition but are less convenient for frequent checking.

Windfalls should be eaten, cooked or preserved in some way as soon as possible. They should never be left to rot under the tree as the rot can spread to the tree itself and affect the next year's crop. If you use windfalls in recipes that call for a certain weight of apples, weigh them after you have cut out the bad bits but before you peel and core them.

FREEZING APPLE SLICES

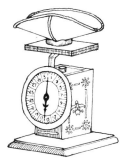

Only firm-textured, well flavoured apples freeze success-fully in slices. Soft-textured varieties are better frozen puréed.

Measure 2 pts (1.1 l) of cold water and 1 tblsp (15 ml) salt into a large bowl. Peel, core and slice the apples into the salted water and stir to prevent them going brown. Rinse about 8 oz (225 g) at a time in cold water and blanch in boiling water for 1 minute only. Cool in cold running water and pat dry with kitchen paper.

The slices can then be frozen in free-flow packs, in dry sugar packs or in sugar syrup. Pack them in manageable quantities and if you use several varieties of apples keep them separate and mark the variety on the label. Different methods of preserving suit different apples, and you can only find out which way suits your apples by trial and error.

1. For free-flow packs spread the blanched apple slices on trays, freeze and when fully frozen, bag, weigh, seal and label. They can be used straight from the freezer as they do not stick together and can be used in any sweet or savoury recipe that calls for apple slices.

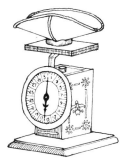

2. For dry-sugar packs you will need approximately 8 oz (225 g) of granulated sugar for every 2 lb (900 g) apples. Sprinkle a layer of sugar in the base of small plastic containers, arrange the blanched apple slices on top and cover with more sugar. Seal, label and freeze.

3. For sugar syrup place 8 oz (225 g) sugar in a pan with 1 pt (600 ml) water and cook over a medium heat for 7 to 8 minutes, shaking the pan occasionally. Do not stir or the sugar will crystallise. Bring to the boil and boil for a further minute. Remove from the heat, add 2 tsp (10 ml) lemon juice and allow to cool completely. When cold, add 2 lb (900 g) prepared apple slices and pour the mixture into small plastic containers leaving a 1 in (2.5 cm) gap at the top to allow room for expansion. Crumple up a sheet of greaseproof paper and place it over the top of the fruit. The apples float in the syrup and the paper pushes them down and stops them discolouring. Cover, label and freeze.

FREEZING APPLE PURÉE

Cooking apples like Bramleys make a tart fluffy purée and eating apples make a firmer and naturally sweeter purée. We find it easier to freeze purée unsweetened and add sugar to taste as needed.

To make the purée: chop whole apples with their skins and cores and sieve them once they are cooked. Alternatively peel and core them first and just mash them with a wooden spoon when they are cooked. Either way you should simmer them in a covered pan with approximately 4 tblsp (60 ml) of water to each 1 lb (450 g) of apples for about 10 minutes until they are soft and mushy, and leave to cool. (Wine, cider or fruit juice may be used instead of water; they all work well.) Measure the cold purée into convenient sized containers leaving about 1 in (2.5 cm) at the top to allow for expansion during freezing. Label and freeze.

Apple purée can also be made in a microwave oven which cuts out a bit of washing up. Peel, core and slice the apples into a container suitable for both microwave and freezer. Add the measured quantity of liquid, cover with plastic cling wrap, prick the wrap with a fork and cook at full power for 2 minutes. Shake the container and cook for a further 2 minutes. Remove the cling wrap and mash the apples with a fork. Allow to cool completely, then cover, label and freeze.

BOTTLING APPLES

Apples can be bottled successfully in slices or in purée. If you do not have proper bottling jars you can use ordinary jam jars and a piece of plastic preserving skin, available from most hardware stores, cut into circles 2 in (5 cm) larger than the top of the jars.

BOTTLING SLICES AND PURÉE

Peel, core and slice the apples into 1½ pts (850 ml) of cold water, add 1 tsp (5 ml) salt and stir well to mix. Bring a large pan of water to the boil and remove from the heat. Drain and rinse approximately 8 oz (225 g) slices at a time in cold water, place them in a sieve and stand it in the boiled water for 2 to 3 minutes until the slices feel pliable but not soft. Pat dry on kitchen paper and pack well into warm dry jars. Make a sugar syrup using 1 lb (450 g) sugar to 1 pt (600 ml) water. Pour the syrup over the fruit to cover and cover the jars.

For purée, spoon into warm dry jars up to the rim, and cover.

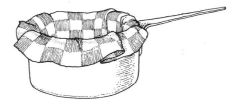

Line the base of a large pan with a folded tea towel to prevent the jars rattling around. Place the jars of slices or purée in the pan leaving about 2 in (5 cm) between them and cover with cold water. Bring the water to the boil very slowly over a medium heat. Reduce the heat and simmer for 20 minutes. Remove the jars, cool and store in a cool, dry cupboard. Once opened store in the refrigerator for up to 2 weeks.

DRYING APPLE RINGS

Apples can also be dried and stored for up to one year. As they shrink considerably, large apples work best. Peel, core and cut the apples into even slices just under $\frac{1}{2}$ inch (1 cm) thick. Dissolve 1 tblsp (15 ml) salt in 2 pints (1.1 l) cold water and soak the apple rings for 15 minutes. Drain and spread on baking sheets. Dry in a very low oven for around 8 hours until shrivelled, leathery and slightly translucent. Cool on racks and store in airtight tins. To reconstitute: soak in cold water, cider or apple juice for one hour.

PECTIN STOCK

Apples, particularly sour cooking apples, are rich in pectin, an essential ingredient for making jams and jellies set. A simple stock can be made from either whole apples or a mixture of whole apples and the skins and cores left over from preparing apples. It can be used to help set fruits such as cherries and strawberries which are low in pectin.

To make approximately 2 pts (1.1 l) of stock cut up 4 lb (1.8 kg) cooking apples and place them in a pan with 4 pts (2.3 l) water. Bring to the boil and simmer gently for 25 to 30 minutes until the apples are very soft and pulpy. Sterilise a jelly bag, place it in a large bowl and pour the apples and juice into the bag. Hang the bag somewhere safe, with the bowl underneath, for at least 2 hours to allow the juice to drip through.

Measure the juice in $\frac{1}{2}$ pt (300 ml) quantities into warm, dry jars or bottles, leaving a $\frac{1}{2}$ in (1 cm) space at the top. Seal and place the jars or bottles in a pan of boiling water with a folded tea towel placed at the bottom to prevent the jars rattling. Boil for 5 minutes to sterilise. Remove from the pan, cool, label and store in a cool, dark cupboard.

A little goes a long way; $\frac{1}{2}$ pt (300 ml) should be sufficient to set 4 lb (1.8 kg) of low pectin fruit for jam or jelly and should be added at the start of cooking. Alternatively it can be added to rescue a jam which refuses to set after it has been boiled with sugar. The quantity will depend on the type of fruit but try $\frac{1}{2}$ pt (300 ml) to 6 lb (2.7 kg) of fruit, reboil for 5 minutes and test again for set.

COOKING WITH APPLES

We have tried out literally hundreds of recipes, and as we experimented have found many new ways of cooking apples. Although we have included some of the great classic apple dishes — apple strudel, for instance, is too good to leave out — we have not thought it necessary to reproduce all the standard apple recipes, which can readily be found elsewhere. The emphasis is very much on original ideas.

Anyone with a surplus of apples will find this book full of new ways to enjoy them, but we have not written solely for them. Many of the recipes use only one or two apples, but it is the addition of the apples that gives these dishes their distinctive flavour.

Apples vary enormously in taste and texture and the ideal apple for one recipe may well be quite unsuitable for another. It would have been pointless to try to specify particular varieties for each recipe. What we have done is to say what type of apples should be used in each case.

Apples are divided into two types, cooking and eating. Eating apples can be cooked but cooking apples are too sour to eat raw. There are hundreds of different apple varieties, and it is well worth trying out unfamiliar ones and extending one's choice.

The cooking apple is large and sour, and fluffs up when it is cooked. It is good for any recipe in which the apples should be puréed and in which sugar is to be added or where other ingredients balance its acidity, but should never be used in any recipe where the apple needs to retain its shape. The most popular British cooking apple is the Bramley which we have used in all the recipes specifying a 'cooking apple'.

Eating apples can be divided into tart and sweet. We have generally used either Coxes or Golden Delicious for recipes calling for 'sweet eating apples' as they both cook well and are the most commonly available in Britain. We would not, however, use excessively sweet apples in savoury recipes. For 'tart eating apples' we have used Granny Smiths.

We have usually stated numbers of apples rather than weights, as a slice or two more or less makes little difference. A small eating apple weighs around 3 oz (75 g), a medium-sized one 4 oz to 5 oz (125 g to 150 g) and a large one seldom weighs much over 6 oz (175 g). Cooking apples are generally larger, a small one weighs between 6 oz and 8 oz (175 g to 225 g), a medium-sized one around 12 oz (350 g) and a large one about 1 lb (450 g).

We have tried, where possible, to take advantage of the natural sweetness in apples and when it is practical have used sweet apples rather than adding sugar to sour ones.

Spoon measurements are level and, at the risk of stating the obvious, we urge you to use either the metric *or* the imperial measurements, not a combination of both.

SOUPS

SPINACH AND APPLE SOUP WITH NUTMEG
serves 4

A creamy soup with a vivid green colour and a beautiful flavour. If fresh spinach isn't available, use an 8 oz (227 g) packet of frozen leaf spinach instead.

1 lb (450 g) fresh spinach
2 sweet eating apples
1 medium-sized onion
2 oz (50 g) butter
$\frac{1}{4}$ tsp (1.25 ml) ground nutmeg
$1\frac{1}{2}$ pt (900 ml) chicken stock
$\frac{3}{4}$ pt (450 ml) milk
$\frac{1}{2}$ tsp (2.5 ml) salt
freshly ground black pepper
2 tsp (10 ml) grated lemon rind
fried bread croutons to garnish

Wash the spinach and discard any tough stems and damaged leaves. Peel, core and quarter the apples. Peel and roughly chop the onion.

Melt the butter in a large pan and add the spinach, apples and onion. Cover and cook over a medium heat for 10 minutes, shaking the pan occasionally to prevent the soup sticking. Add the nutmeg and stock, cover and simmer for 30 minutes.

Liquidise until smooth. Return the soup to the pan and reheat. Add the milk, salt, pepper and lemon rind, bring to the boil and simmer for 5 minutes. Serve hot with croutons scattered on top.

TOMATO, ORANGE AND APPLE SOUP
WITH CORIANDER
serves 6 to 8

This is a super quick and easy soup using canned tomatoes. For a dinner party, float a little freshly grated carrot on top.

$1\frac{1}{2}$ lbs (675 g) cooking apples
1 medium-sized orange
1 pt (600 ml) chicken stock
$1\frac{3}{4}$ lb (794 g) can tomatoes
1 tsp (5 ml) salt
freshly ground black pepper
1 tblsp (15 ml) ground coriander
2 tsp (10 ml) sugar

Peel, core and thickly slice the apples; finely grate the orange rind and squeeze the juice.

Place the apples, orange rind and juice, the stock, tomatoes and their juice, salt, plenty of pepper, coriander and sugar in a large pan. Bring to the boil, cover and simmer for 30 minutes. Liquidise until smooth. Return the soup to the pan and reheat.

HADDOCK, CIDER AND APPLE SOUP
WITH ROSEMARY
serves 4

A most unusual soup, cider-coloured and chunky. If you use fresh rosemary, garnish each bowl with a tiny sprig just before serving. Serve with well buttered crusty white bread.

1 large onion
2 tart eating apples
1 lb (450 g) fillet of haddock
$\frac{1}{2}$ oz (15 g) butter
$\frac{1}{2}$ pt (300 ml) fish or chicken stock
1 pt (600 ml) strong dry cider
good sprig fresh rosemary or
$\frac{1}{2}$ tsp (2.5 ml) dried
salt and freshly ground black pepper
2 oz (50 g) fresh peeled prawns

Peel and finely chop the onion; peel, core and finely chop the apples and cut the haddock into small chunks.

Melt the butter in a pan, add the chopped onion and cook for 5 minutes over a medium heat until the onion is softened but not browned. Add the chopped apple and cook for a minute.

Add the haddock, stock, cider, rosemary, salt and plenty of pepper. Bring to the boil, cover and simmer gently for 30 minutes. Remove the sprig of rosemary if fresh is used and add the prawns. Simmer for 2 to 3 minutes and serve hot.

CURRIED OXTAIL AND APPLE SOUP
serves 6 to 8

Prepare this rich, dark soup in advance so that the surplus fat can be skimmed from the surface whilst the soup is cool.

2 lb (900 g) lean oxtail
2 large carrots
1 small swede
2 medium-sized onions
2 large sweet eating apples
1 medium-sized lemon
2 tblsp (30 ml) plain flour
1 tblsp (15 ml) madras curry powder
1 tsp (5 ml) salt
freshly ground black pepper
3 pt (1.7 l) beef stock

Place the oxtail in a large pan with no extra fat and cook over a medium heat for 10 minutes turning occasionally to prevent sticking, until the meat is golden brown all round.

Scrape and coarsely chop the carrots; peel and coarsely chop the swede and onions; peel, core and thickly slice the apples; finely grate the lemon rind and squeeze the juice.

Add the carrot, swede, onion and apple to the oxtail and cook for a further 5 minutes, stirring continuously until lightly browned. Add the lemon rind and juice, the flour, curry powder, salt, pepper and stock and stir well. Bring to the boil, reduce the heat, cover and simmer gently for 1 hour 30 minutes.

Remove the oxtail from the pan; take the meat off the bones and set aside. Discard the bones. Allow the soup to cool completely. Skim the fat from the surface and liquidise the soup until smooth.

Return the soup to the pan and reheat. Chop the reserved oxtail into small pieces and add to the soup. Simmer for 5 minutes and serve hot.

APPLE VICHYSSOISE
serves 3 to 4

A delicious fresh-tasting creamy soup which is equally good hot or cold. If you serve the soup cold give it a good stir and pour it into bowls at the last moment.

1 medium-sized potato
1 medium-sized onion
1 oz (25 g) butter
1 pt (600 ml) water
salt and freshly ground black pepper
sprig of parsley
2 small sweet eating apples
4 tblsp (60 ml) fresh single cream
2 tblsp (30 ml) finely chopped chives

Peel and slice the potato and onion. Melt the butter in a pan. Add the potatoes and onions and stir over a gentle heat for a few minutes. Add the water, plenty of salt, pepper and parsley, cover and simmer for 10 minutes.

Peel, core and slice the apples, and add them to the potatoes and onions. Continue cooking for approximately 10 minutes until all the vegetables are soft. Remove the parsley and liquidise until smooth.

Serve hot or cold with a spoonful of cream swirled into each bowl and a sprinkling of finely chopped chives.

CHILLED APPLE AND COURGETTE SOUP
serves 3 to 4

A light refreshing soup which could be made with end of season 'overgrown' courgettes, in which case the courgettes should be weighed without their cores. Make the soup in advance to give it time to chill thoroughly.

**8 oz (225 g) courgettes
2 sweet eating apples
1 pt (600 ml) water
large pinch of salt
4 tblsp (60 ml) fresh single cream
2 tblsp (30 ml) finely chopped spring onions**

Wash and trim the courgettes, and slice them into a pan. Peel, core and slice the apples and add them to the courgettes with the water and salt. Cover and simmer for 10–15 minutes until the courgettes and apples are soft. Liquidise until smooth and chill.

Stir well and ladle into bowls. Spoon a little cream on to the soup and scatter with the spring onions.

STARTERS

CHEESE, SMOKED HAM AND APPLE SOUFFLÉ
serves 4

For a super savoury supper dish this one is hard to beat.
You can make up the thick cheesy sauce in advance and
fold in the whisked eggs just before cooking.

1 oz (25 g) butter
1 oz (25 g) plain flour
¼ pt (125 ml) milk
4 oz (125 g) mature Cheddar cheese
1 tart eating apple
1 medium-sized onion
2 oz (50 g) smoked ham
salt and freshly ground black pepper
2 eggs
butter for greasing

Oven temperature 375°F, 190°C, Gas Mark 5
Melt the butter in a pan over a medium heat and stir in the
plain flour. Cook for a minute, then stir in the milk, a little
at a time to make a smooth sauce. Bring to the boil,
stirring continuously and allow the sauce to boil for a
minute. (It will be very thick.) Remove the pan from the
heat and allow to cool slightly.

Coarsely grate the cheese; peel, core and coarsely grate
the apple; peel and coarsely grate the onion and roughly
chop the ham. Add the cheese, apple, onion and ham to
the sauce with salt and plenty of pepper and stir well.

Separate the eggs and place the yolks in the sauce and
the whites in a large bowl. Whisk the egg whites until stiff
but not dry and fold into the sauce.

Butter a 2 pt (1.1 l) soufflé dish and gently pour in the mixture. Cook on the top shelf of the preheated oven for 45 minutes or until well risen and the soufflé sets in a golden crust. Serve immediately with hot buttered toast.

AVOCADO AND APPLE DIP
makes about 1 pt (600 ml)

Leave the stones in the dip until just before serving as it stops the avocado from discolouring. This recipe makes a party-sized quantity. If you can't get limes use lemon juice to taste instead.

1 lb (450 g) cooking apples
1 lime
2 medium-sized ripe avocados
salt and freshly ground black pepper
4 drops of Tabasco
8 oz (225 g) full fat soft cheese

Peel, core and slice the apples into a pan. Finely grate the rind from the lime and squeeze the juice. Add the rind and juice to the apple and cook for 10 to 15 minutes over a medium heat, shaking the pan occasionally to prevent sticking. Beat well to a purée and allow to cool.

Cut the avocados in half, twist to separate and remove the stones. Scoop out the flesh with a teaspoon into the cooled apple purée. Add salt, pepper and Tabasco and stir well.

Liquidise the apple and avocado mixture with the cream cheese until smooth. Divide between two serving dishes, bury one stone in each dish, and cover with cling film until required.

SOUSED CIDERED HERRING
makes 12 rolls

This is a lovely, lightly spiced recipe for herring. They keep well for up to 1 week, covered with cling film and stored in the refrigerator. Serve them with lettuce and brown bread as a starter or mix with potatoes, chopped red-skinned apple and mayonnaise to make a moist, main meal mixed salad.

**6 medium-sized herring fillets (about
6 oz (175g) each)
salt and freshly ground black pepper
2 small onions
1 small orange
$\frac{3}{4}$ pt (450 ml) strong dry cider
$\frac{1}{4}$ pt (150 ml) dark malt vinegar
12 dried allspice berries
12 cloves
12 whole black peppercorns
butter for greasing**

Oven temperature 350°F, 180°C, Gas Mark 4
Rinse the herring fillets and pat dry with kitchen paper. Place them skin side down on a work surface and season well with salt and pepper.

Roll up from the tail end, secure with a cocktail stick and place in a 3 pt (1.7 l) ovenproof dish. Peel and thinly slice the onions and pare the rind from the orange using a sharp knife. Add the onion, orange rind, cider, vinegar, allspice berries, cloves and peppercorns to the herring fillets. Butter a large sheet of foil and cover the dish. Bake in the centre of the preheated oven for 45 minutes and allow to cool in the dish.

BLUE CHEESE AND APPLE QUICHE ON WALNUT PASTRY
serves 4

A superb quiche with an unusual nutty pastry and a melt in the mouth filling! It is best served piping hot, straight from the oven.

Pastry
8 oz (200 g) wholemeal flour
pinch of salt
4 oz (100 g) butter
2 oz (50 g) walnut pieces
1 egg

Filling
6 oz (175 g) Lymeswold cheese
6 oz (175 g) Dolcelatte
4 oz (100 g) smoked ham
2 small sweet eating apples
2 tblsp (30 ml) milk
1 tsp (5 ml) caster sugar
salt and freshly ground black pepper
2 eggs

Oven temperature 400°F, 200°C, Gas Mark 6

To make the pastry: place the flour and salt in a bowl. Add the butter, cut into small pieces and rub in with the fingertips until the mixture resembles breadcrumbs. Finely chop the walnuts and stir in. Lightly beat the egg and mix well to a firm dough. Roll the pastry out to a large circle $\frac{1}{4}$ in ($\frac{1}{2}$ cm) thick and line an 8 in (20 cm) fluted flan tin. Prick the base with a fork and chill for 30 minutes. Place the flan tin on a baking sheet, cover the pastry base with a sheet of greaseproof paper, fill with dried beans and bake blind for 10 minutes. Remove the paper and beans and bake for a further 10 minutes. Reduce heat to 350°F, 180°C, Gas Mark 4.

To make the filling: remove the rind from the cheeses and cut into small pieces; trim the fat from the ham and chop; peel, core and finely chop the apples. Place the cheese, ham and apples in a heatproof bowl with the milk, sugar, salt and plenty of pepper. Place the bowl over a pan of boiling water and stir gently until the cheese has melted. Remove from the heat, lightly whisk the eggs and stir in. Pour the mixture into the pastry case and bake in the centre of the preheated oven for 40 to 45 minutes or until the filling is well risen and dark golden.

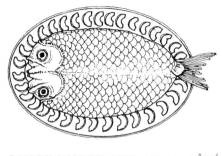

QUICK KIPPER AND APPLE PÂTÉ
serves 4

You don't use a lot of apples in this recipe but they do add something to this simple pâté and make it go further. It will keep covered for up to 1 week in the refrigerator.

8 oz (225 g) kipper fillets
6 oz (175 g) cream cheese
2 tsp (10 ml) lemon juice
$\frac{1}{2}$ tsp (2.5 ml) salt
freshly ground black pepper
6 tblsp (90 ml) apple purée (from
1 medium-sized eating apple)

Preheat the grill to high and cook the kipper fillets for 5 to 7 minutes until the fish flakes easily. Scrape the flesh from the skin and discard any remaining large bones. Allow to cool.

Place the kipper flesh, cream cheese, lemon juice, salt, pepper and apple purée in a bowl and beat well until blended.

Spoon into a small bowl or individual ramekins and allow to chill before serving with hot buttery toast.

37

FISH

SOLE WITH PRAWNS, BACON AND APPLES
serves 4

This is a super, sweet and salty topping which can be used just as successfully on any white fish.

4 fillets of sole
salt and freshly ground black pepper
4 tsp (20 ml) lemon juice

Topping
8 oz (225 g) smoked streaky bacon
2 sweet eating apples
2 oz (50 g) butter
8 oz (225 g) peeled prawns

Season the fish with salt, pepper and lemon juice; place them on a sheet of foil and grill for 10 to 12 minutes or until the fish leaves the skin easily.

To make the topping: remove the rind and any bone from the bacon and cut into small pieces. Cook in a frying pan with no extra fat for 5 minutes or until crispy and golden.

Peel, core and chop the apple into small pieces and add to the bacon with the butter. Fry quickly for 2 to 3 minutes or until the apple is golden but still holding its shape. Add the prawns and cook a further minute to heat through. Season with pepper. Divide the topping between the fish and spread over. Serve hot.

COD AND RAISIN PIE WITH PUFF THATCH
serves 4

This is a good way to turn an everyday fish into a special
dish. Add 2 tblsp (30 ml) calvados or brandy to the cream
to make it extra rich.

1 large onion
1 lb (450 g) cod fillet
1 oz (25 g) butter
2 oz (50 g) raisins
$\frac{1}{4}$ pt (150 ml) dry cider
salt and freshly ground black pepper
1 lb (450 g) cooking apples
8 oz (227 g) packet frozen puff pastry,
thawed
milk to glaze
$\frac{1}{4}$ pt (142 ml) carton fresh single cream

Oven temperature 400°F, 200°C, Gas Mark 6

Peel and finely slice the onion; skin the cod and cut into chunks. Melt the butter in a pan and add the onions and raisins. Cook over a medium heat for 7 to 8 minutes until the onions are softened and lightly browned. Add the cod, cider, plenty of salt and pepper, cover and simmer gently for 10 minutes. Transfer to a 3 pt (1.7 l) pie dish. Peel, core and slice the apples and stir into the fish mixture.

Roll out the pastry to an oblong 1 in (2.5 cm) larger all the way round than the pie dish. Cut off a 1 in (2.5 cm) strip from the outside edge, brush the rim of pie dish with milk and press on the pastry strip. Brush with milk and arrange the pastry lid on top, pressing down lightly to seal. Mark a criss cross pattern all over the pastry, using a sharp knife and mark a pattern round the edge. Make a hole in the centre for the steam to escape and brush with milk.

Bake in the centre of the preheated oven for 25 minutes until the pastry is well risen and golden brown. Remove from oven, pour the cream through the hole and shake the dish gently to combine. Serve hot with boiled potatoes.

DEEP-FRIED MONKFISH IN APPLE BATTER
serves 4

Use a sieved apple purée to make this batter and the tartare apple sauce (on page 92) to go with it. The batter is beautifully light and crisp and can be used for onion rings, tiny cauliflower florets and cubes of cheese with equal success.

Batter
4 oz (125 g) plain flour
2 tsp (10 ml) baking powder
$\frac{1}{2}$ tsp (2.5 ml) salt
freshly ground black pepper
$\frac{1}{4}$ pt (150 ml) sieved apple purée (made from 1 large cooking apple)
4 tblsp (60 ml) cider
1 egg

Fish
1 lb (450 g) monkfish tail
2 tblsp (30 ml) lemon juice
2 tblsp (30 ml) seasoned flour
oil for frying

To make the batter: sieve the flour, baking powder, salt and pepper into a bowl. Add the apple purée, cider and egg and beat well together for 1 to 2 minutes.

Remove the skin and main bone from the monkfish, cut into 20 chunks and place in a bowl with the lemon juice. Mix well and coat in seasoned flour.

Dip the monkfish in batter and drop 5 pieces at a time gently into hot oil. Shake the basket and cook for 1 minute until dark golden. Drain on kitchen paper and keep warm. Repeat with remaining monkfish and serve immediately with tartare apple sauce.

COD IN CREAMY COCONUT
AND APPLE SAUCE
serves 4

This is a mild creamy curry that makes an everyday fish into something quite special. Serve with plain boiled rice mixed with peas.

1 large onion
2 tblsp (30 ml) oil
2 medium-sized cooking apples
3 oz (75 g) creamed coconut
1 tsp (5 ml) salt
1 tsp (5 ml) sugar
$\frac{1}{2}$ pt (300 ml) chicken stock
2 tsp (10 ml) madras curry powder
2 tsp (10 ml) ground coriander
1 tsp (5 ml) ground cumin
$1\frac{1}{2}$ lb (675 g) fillet of cod

Peel and finely chop the onion. Place the oil in a large pan, add the onion and cook over a medium heat for 5 to 7 minutes until the onion is softened and lightly browned. Peel, core and slice the apple into the pan and coarsely chop the coconut. Add the coconut to the pan with the salt, sugar, stock, curry powder, coriander and cumin. Bring to the boil, cover and simmer for 20 minutes, stirring occasionally to prevent sticking. Liquidise until smooth and return to the pan. Skin the cod and cut into large chunks. Add to the sauce and simmer uncovered for 10 minutes until the cod flakes easily when pressed with a knife.

VEGETABLES

LITTLE SPINACH AND APPLE PANCAKES
serves 4 to 6

These little pancakes, similar to gnocchi, are a delicious accompaniment to any plainly cooked meat dish. They are prepared in advance up to the final quick cooking in hot oil.

1 lb (450 g) spinach
2 sweet eating apples
8 oz (225 g) cream cheese
salt and freshly ground black pepper
2 beaten eggs
6 tblsp (90 ml) flour
oil

Wash the spinach thoroughly and remove stalks. Peel, core and finely chop the apples. Place together in a pan with a little water and cook for 10 minutes over a medium heat until they are soft. Mash them well with the back of a wooden spoon and continue cooking, still stirring, to evaporate the water. Stir in the cream cheese and cook a minute or two longer. Season to taste with salt and pepper.

Transfer to a bowl, add the beaten eggs, stir them in well and lastly fold in the flour. Set aside to cool.

Heat a little oil in a heavy frying pan. Drop small spoonfuls of the mixture into the pan, a few at a time, allowing room between each for them to spread. Turn when golden and cook the other side. Serve hot.

SWEETCORN AND APPLE FRITTERS
makes 10

Serve these light, crumbly fritters with deep fried chicken pieces or grilled bacon. They cook like dropped scones but if you don't have a griddle use a large non-stick frying pan instead.

**2 large fresh corn-on-the-cob
1 tart eating apple
1 medium-sized onion
4 tblsp (60 ml) self-raising flour
$\frac{1}{2}$ tsp (2.5 ml) salt
freshly ground black pepper
$\frac{1}{2}$ tsp (2.5 ml) caster sugar
$\frac{1}{4}$ pt (142 ml) carton fresh double cream
butter for greasing**

Strip off the outer leaves of the corn-on-the-cob and pull away the silky threads. Rinse the cob and scrape the kernels into a bowl. Peel, core and finely dice the apple; peel and finely chop the onion. Add the apple and onion to the corn. Sieve in the flour, salt, pepper and sugar. Pour in the cream and stir well to make a stiff batter.

Lightly grease a griddle with butter and heat for 2 to 3 minutes. Drop spoonfuls of the batter on to the griddle, well spaced apart, and cook for 1 to 2 minutes or until they begin to set round the outside edge and the underside is golden. Turn the fritters over with a fish slice and cook the second side for 1 to 2 minutes. Transfer to the serving dish and keep warm. Repeat with the remaining batter.

APPLE AND POTATO GRATIN

Delicious and almost a meal in itself for 2 to 3 people. As an accompaniment to a plain roast, grill or sausages it would serve 4 to 6.

1 lb (450 g) firm (preferably new) potatoes
4 oz (100 g) bacon
2 oz (50 g) butter
2 tart eating apples
salt and freshly ground black pepper
2 tblsp (30 ml) dry cider
$\frac{1}{4}$ pt (142 ml) carton fresh double cream

Oven temperature 400°F, 200°C, Gas Mark 6
Peel the potatoes, parboil them for 10 minutes, drain and allow to cool slightly. Cut the bacon into small pieces and lightly fry them in 1 oz (25 g) of the butter until golden, and set aside. Melt the remaining 1 oz (25 g) of butter. Peel, core and slice the apples and toss them in the butter.

Butter an ovenproof dish. Finely slice the potatoes and arrange layers of potatoes, apples and bacon in the dish, ending with a layer of potatoes. Sprinkle each layer meanly with salt and generously with pepper. Pour over any buttery juices from the bacon and apple pan. Pour in the cider and cover loosely with a sheet of greaseproof paper. Bake in the preheated oven for 30 minutes. Pour in the cream and cook uncovered for a further 10 minutes. Serve hot.

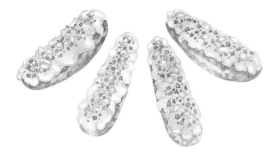

BAKED COURGETTES WITH CHEESE AND APPLE STUFFING
serves 6

Apples go surprisingly well with courgettes and the filling for this recipe can be prepared in advance.

6 medium-sized courgettes
2 sweet eating apples
2 oz (50 g) butter
2 cloves garlic
2 tblsp (30 ml) chopped parsley
salt and freshly ground black pepper
2 oz (50 g) cream cheese

Oven temperature 400°F, 200°C, Gas Mark 6
Wash and trim the courgettes, and simmer them in salted water for 7 minutes. Drain and allow them to cool. Peel, core and grate the apples. Melt the butter in a frying pan and cook the apples over a low heat for 5 minutes until they begin to soften.

Cut the courgettes in half. Scoop out the centre of each courgette to approximately $\frac{1}{4}$ in ($\frac{1}{2}$ cm) of the skin and chop finely. Add to the apples and continue cooking, stirring frequently until both are tender. Peel and crush the garlic and add with the chopped parsley, salt and pepper. Mash well with the back of a wooden spoon so that the mixture is almost a purée. Stir in the cream cheese and continue cooking until it has melted and is thoroughly mixed.

Butter an ovenproof dish just large enough to hold the courgette halves in one layer. Fill the centre of each courgette half with the apple mixture, pack it in firmly and smooth the tops. Bake in the centre of the preheated oven for 45 minutes.

PUMPKIN AND APPLE PURÉE
serves 4

This odd sounding mixture is good with game or turkey.

**1 lb (450 g) pumpkin, weighed when
peeled and cored
3 tart eating apples
1 oz (25 g) butter
salt and freshly ground black pepper
good pinch of dried oregano**

Chop the pumpkin into rough cubes and steam for approximately 20 minutes. (If you don't have a proper steamer rest a colander over a pan of boiling water.) Peel, core and slice the apples, add them to the pumpkin and steam for a further 5 minutes until both the pumpkin and the apples are soft.

Transfer the vegetables to a saucepan and mash them well with a fork. Add the butter, salt and pepper and allow the purée to 'bubble' gently over a low heat to evaporate any surplus liquid. Add the oregano and taste for seasoning. Serve hot.

BRAISED RED CABBAGE WITH APPLE
serves 4 to 6

A good hearty vegetable dish which goes particularly well with pork on a cold winter's day.

**1½ lb (675 g) red cabbage
1 medium-sized onion
2 tblsp (30 ml) oil
2 tblsp (30 ml) cider or wine vinegar
salt and freshly ground black pepper
1 large cooking apple
8 fl oz (225 ml) dry cider or wine
1 tblsp (15 ml) brown sugar
fresh chopped parsley to garnish**

Remove the coarse outside leaves and centre core from the cabbage and slice finely. Peel and chop the onion, heat the oil in a large pan and cook the onions for 5 minutes over medium heat to soften but not brown. Add the vinegar and cabbage, season with salt and pepper and continue cooking over a gentle heat, stirring from time to time.

Peel, core and slice the apple into the pan. Add the cider or wine and the sugar. Stir well, cover and cook over a gentle heat for 1 hour to 1 hour 20 minutes or until the cabbage is tender. Serve sprinkled with chopped parsley.

SALADS

BEETROOT AND APPLE SALAD WITH BLUE CHEESE DRESSING
serves 4

Beetroot stains everything a purply pink and this speedy salad is no exception. Use boiled beetroot rather than pickled. Decorate with the lumpfish roe if you are entertaining. You can buy it in most supermarkets; it's not too expensive but looks terrific.

1 medium-sized onion
2 oz (50 g) shelled hazelnuts
2 medium-sized carrots
2 tart eating apples
2 small cooked beetroots
salt and freshly ground black pepper

Dressing
$\frac{1}{4}$ pt (142 ml) carton fresh soured cream
4 tblsp (60 ml) mayonnaise
6 tblsp (90 ml) milk
3 oz (75 g) Danish Blue cheese
1 red-skinned apple
1 small jar of black lumpfish roe

Peel and very thinly slice the onion, coarsely chop the hazelnuts, scrape and coarsely grate the carrots. Peel, core and coarsely grate the apples and coarsely grate the beetroot. Place the onion, hazelnuts, carrot, apple and beetroot in a large bowl and season well with salt and pepper.

To make the dressing: spoon the sour cream into a

49

bowl with the mayonnaise and the milk. Crumble in the blue cheese and beat well to mix. Add half the dressing to the salad and toss all the ingredients well. Spoon into the serving bowl and top with the remaining dressing.

Core the apple and cut into 8 slices. Arrange the slices over the dressing and place a small teaspoonful of the lumpfish roe in between each. Serve immediately.

CHICORY AND APPLE SALAD
serves 3 to 4

An attractive salad to serve as part of a cold buffet, with an unusual lemon, cream and mustard dressing.

6 oz (175 g) chicory
1 large sweet eating apple
freshly ground black pepper
$\frac{1}{2}$ oz (15 g) shelled walnuts

Dressing
1 tblsp (15 ml) lemon juice
$\frac{1}{2}$ tsp (2.5 ml) mild mustard
3 tblsp (45 ml) double cream
salt

Cut the chicory into 1 in (2.5 cm) lengths and place them in a salad bowl. Peel, core and chop the apple into small pieces. Arrange the apple pieces in the centre of the chicory and sprinkle with black pepper. Pile the nuts on top.

To make the dressing: mix the lemon juice with the mustard and the cream, add a little salt and pour over the salad.

RICE, PEANUT AND APPLE SALAD
WITH CHICKEN
serves 4 to 6

This makes leftover chicken spin out into another meal.
Choose a quality vinegar for the dressing.

8 oz (225 g) long grain rice
4 oz (100 g) frozen sweetcorn
2 sticks of celery
1 medium-sized red pepper
2 oz (50 g) salted peanuts
2 small tart eating apples
12 oz (350 g) cooked chicken
2 oz (50 g) sultanas

Dressing
8 tblsp (120 ml) olive oil
4 tblsp (60 ml) tarragon vinegar
$\frac{1}{2}$ tsp (2.5 ml) salt
freshly ground black pepper
$\frac{1}{2}$ tsp (2.5 ml) Dijon mustard

Bring a large pan of salted water to the boil, add the rice and simmer uncovered for 5 minutes. Add the frozen sweetcorn, return to the boil and simmer for a further 5 minutes. Drain through a sieve and rinse in running water until cold. The rice should still have a bite to it and the grains should all be separate.

Wash and finely chop the celery, cut the pepper in half, remove the seeds, core and finely chop; coarsely chop the peanuts; peel, core and finely chop the apples into small pieces and cut the chicken into bite-sized chunks.

Place the rice and sweetcorn in a large bowl and add the celery, pepper, peanuts, apple, chicken and sultanas. Stir with a fork to mix.

To make the dressing: pour the oil and vinegar into a screw-top jar. Add the salt, pepper and mustard and shake the jar well to mix. Pour the dressing over the rice and stir well.

CARROT AND APPLE SALAD WITH CREAM CHEESE AND WALNUT DRESSING
serves 4 to 6

Don't make this salad too long before serving. The walnut flavouring should be subtle rather than overpowering.

4 oz (100 g) cream cheese
5 tsp (25 ml) wine vinegar
3 tblsp (45 ml) oil
6 to 8 shelled walnut pieces
2 sweet eating apples
2 medium-sized carrots
Salt and freshly ground black pepper

Mix the cream cheese with the vinegar in a large bowl and whisk in the oil. Finely chop and add the walnuts.

Peel and grate the apples and carrots into the bowl and mix very thoroughly. Season with salt and pepper.

CABBAGE AND APPLE SALAD
serves 4

Despite the 'ordinariness' of its ingredients this is an exceptionally refreshing salad. It is also very pretty with its variety of pale greens. Use plenty of parsley to enhance the colours. The dressing is a simple vinaigrette with just a touch of mustard.

**8 oz (225 g) green cabbage weighed without
its outside leaves
1 tsp (5 ml) mild French mustard such as
Grey de Poupon
1 tblsp (15 ml) wine vinegar
3 tblsp (45 ml) oil
salt and freshly ground black pepper
2 large tart eating apples
1 tblsp (15 ml) fresh chopped parsley**

Finely slice the cabbage. Mix the mustard and vinegar together in a salad bowl, stir in the oil, salt and pepper and add the cabbage. Peel, core and coarsely grate the apple directly into the cabbage. Add the parsley, toss immediately and serve as soon as possible.

BEEF AND LAMB

BEEF, BACON AND CHESTNUT POT WITH GREEN PEPPERCORNS
serves 4 to 6

It's worth using fresh chestnuts for this rich autumnal casserole but you can use reconstituted dried ones or canned ones instead. It cooks to a thick spicy gravy and the flavour improves overnight.

2 large onions
6 oz (175 g) back bacon
4 tblsp (60 ml) oil
3 lb (1.4 kg) lean leg of beef
1½ lb (675 g) cooking apples
1 tsp (5 ml) dried green peppercorns or 2 tsp
(10 ml) green peppercorns in brine, drained
12 whole allspice berries
1 tsp (5 ml) salt
¼ pt (150 ml) dry white wine
8 oz (225g) fresh chestnuts
½ tsp (2.5 ml) freshly ground black pepper

Oven temperature 350°F, 180°C, Gas Mark 4
Peel the onions and cut them into large chunks. Cut the rind from the bacon and chop roughly. Heat the oil in a large pan, add the onion and the bacon and fry for 5 to 7 minutes over a medium heat or until lightly browned. Remove the onion and bacon from the pan with a slotted spoon and transfer to a large ovenproof dish.

Cut the beef into large chunks and trim off any surplus fat. Peel and core the apples and cut into large chunks. Fry the beef and the apples for 5 to 7 minutes or until the beef is lightly browned. Transfer to the casserole with the green peppercorns, allspice, salt and wine. Cook in the centre of the preheated oven for 2 hours.

Cut round the middle part of the chestnuts with a sharp knife and grill for 5 minutes or until the skins blacken and split. Take off the hard outer shell and the furry insides, holding each nut with a teatowel. Add the whole chestnuts to the casserole with the pepper, and cook for a further 1 hour or until the meat is tender. Stir the casserole well to break up the apple and serve with baked potatoes.

PARCELS OF BEEF STUFFED WITH APPLES AND PRUNES IN PORT WINE SAUCE
serves 4

One of the most delicious recipes we've tried and now established as a firm favourite. Choose a lean, tender cut of beef such as top side, have it cut thin and beaten even thinner. The prunes should be soaked for several hours in advance.

8 oz (225 g) prunes
8 fl oz (225 ml) port
3 tart eating apples
2 oz (50 g) butter
salt and freshly ground black pepper
pinch of mixed herbs
4 slices of lean beef each weighing 3 oz (75 g)
2 tblsp (30 ml) oil
$\frac{1}{4}$ pt (142 ml) carton of fresh double cream
fresh chopped parsley to decorate

Soak the prunes in the port overnight or for several hours. Strain, stone and chop the prunes but reserve the port for the sauce. Peel, core and coarsely grate the apples. Melt the butter in a pan, add the prunes and apples and stir for a few minutes until the apples have softened. Stir in the salt, pepper and mixed herbs.

Sandwich the beef slices between sheets of greaseproof paper and beat with a meat mallet as thinly as possible without it breaking.

Spread a quarter of the apple-prune mixture on each slice, fold in the ends, roll into parcels and tie with string.

Heat the oil in a small shallow pan. Gently brown the beef parcels all over, cover and cook over a very low heat for 20 to 30 minutes, depending on the tenderness of the meat. Transfer the parcels to a plate, cut away the strings and keep warm.

Discard any surplus fat from the pan. Pour in the reserved port, stir in the cooking juices, strain through a small sieve and return to the pan.

Stir over a high heat until the sauce has lightly thickened and stir in the cream. Add any juices that have collected from the meat. Continue cooking a moment or two longer; the sauce should not be too thick. Pour the sauce over the beef parcels and sprinkle with parsley.

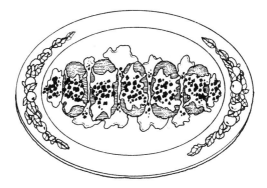

ROAST SHOULDER OF LAMB
WITH APPLE STUFFING
serves 6 to 8

Shoulder of lamb is beautifully flavoured but awkward to carve. An attractive and simple solution is to part-bone the shoulder, removing the flat bone but leaving the knuckle, and stuffing the pocket. The joint looks like a whole shoulder but is much more manageable.

Stuffing
1 onion
2 cloves of garlic
1 oz (25 g) butter
2 oz (50 g) fresh breadcrumbs
8 oz (225 g) cooking apples
1 tsp (5 ml) paprika
1 tblsp (15 ml) fresh chopped parsley
1 tsp (5 ml) thyme
1 tsp (5 ml) rosemary
1 tblsp (15 ml) cream, milk or cider
salt and freshly ground black pepper

4 lb (1.8 kg) shoulder of lamb
1 tsp (5 ml) rosemary
oil to mix
1 medium-sized onion

Oven temperature 375°F, 190°C, Gas Mark 5
To make the stuffing: peel and finely chop the onion. Peel and crush the garlic. Melt the butter in a heavy frying pan, add the onion and cook over a medium heat for about 5 minutes until softened but not browned. Peel, core and coarsely grate the apple into the onions, stirring from time to time to make sure they do not burn. When the

apples have softened stir in the paprika. Place the bread-crumbs in a bowl, add the apples, parsley, thyme, rose-mary, half the garlic, cream, milk or cider, salt and pepper and mix well.

Remove the flat bladebone from the lamb by sliding a sharp knife round the bone and cutting it off at the joint.

Lay the lamb skin side down, remove any surplus fat from inside the joint, fill the pocket with the stuffing and sew up the sides using a large needle and fine string. Do not knot the ends but leave enough string to be able to pull it free when the joint is cooked.

Turn the joint over and remove the skin and shave away any surplus fat with a sharp knife.

Mix the remaining garlic, rosemary, salt and pepper with a little oil and brush this mixture all over the lamb. Peel the onion and roll in a little oil. Place the lamb in a lightly oiled roasting dish, just large enough to hold the lamb and the onion. Cook in the centre of the preheated oven for $1\frac{1}{2}$ hours.

BREAST OF LAMB STUFFED WITH BRAZIL NUTS, APPLES, DATES AND APRICOTS
serves 6

Boned breast of lamb is full of flavour and makes a pretty-coloured slice with this fruit-filled stuffing.

Stuffing
1 tart eating apple
1 small leek
4 oz (125 g) dried apricots
4 oz (125 g) stoned dates
4 oz (125 g) brazil nuts
4 oz (125 g) wholemeal breadcrumbs
2 oz (50 g) butter
salt and freshly ground black pepper

3 lb (1.4 kg) boned breast of lamb

Oven temperature 400°F, 200°C, Gas Mark 6
To make the stuffing: peel and coarsely chop the apple; wash and finely chop the leek; coarsely chop the apricots and dates and finely chop the brazil nuts. Place the apple, leek, apricots, dates and nuts in a bowl with the breadcrumbs. Melt the butter and add to the bowl with salt and plenty of pepper and stir well to mix.

Spoon the stuffing onto the lamb, roll up and tie with string. Wrap the joint in foil and bake in a roasting tin in the centre of the preheated oven for 2 hours. Allow to settle for 10 minutes before carving into thick slices.

SPICED LAMB WITH LEEKS, COURGETTES AND APPLES
serves 6

If you don't want to cook this dish as a casserole you can cook a boned, rolled shoulder of lamb on the bed of vegetables and carve it into thick slices to serve. The flavour is fresh and delicately spiced and improves the second day.

2 lb (900 g) shoulder of lamb
8 oz (225 g) fresh tomatoes
8 oz (225 g) fresh courgettes
1 lb (450 g) cooking apples
2 small leeks
2 tblsp (30 ml) oil
1 pt (600 ml) beef stock
$\frac{1}{2}$ tsp (2.5 ml) cinnamon
$\frac{1}{2}$ tsp (2.5 ml) paprika
1 tblsp (15 ml) ground cumin
1 tblsp (15 ml) ground coriander
2 tsp (10 ml) turmeric
salt and freshly ground black pepper

Oven temperature 350°F, 180°C, Gas Mark 4
Cut the shoulder of lamb into large cubes and trim off any surplus fat. Skin the tomatoes and cut them in half. Cut the courgettes into slices. Peel, core and slice the apples and rinse and slice the leeks.

Heat the oil in a large pan and cook the lamb over a medium heat for 5 to 7 minutes until lightly browned. Remove the lamb from the pan with a slotted spoon and transfer to a large ovenproof dish. Add the courgettes, apples and leeks to the pan and cook for 3 to 4 minutes to brown lightly. Add the tomatoes, the stock, the cinnamon, paprika, cumin, coriander, turmeric, salt and pepper and bring the liquid to the boil.

Pour the mixture over the lamb, cover and cook in the centre of the oven for 2 hours or until the lamb feels tender. Serve with plain boiled rice or potatoes baked in their jackets.

LAMB HOTPOT WITH ROOT VEGETABLES
serves 4

Choose shoulder or leg and cook and serve this recipe in a wide shallow dish.

$1\frac{1}{2}$ lb (675 g) lean lamb
2 tblsp (30 ml) oil
1 tblsp (15 ml) flour
$\frac{1}{4}$ pt (150 ml) stock
$\frac{1}{4}$ pt (150 ml) dry cider
$\frac{1}{4}$ tsp (1.25 ml) tomato purée
generous pinch of rosemary
salt and freshly ground black pepper
1 medium-sized parsnip
1 medium-sized onion
1 clove of garlic
1 small turnip
2 large sweet eating apples
2 oz (50 g) butter
$1\frac{1}{2}$ lb (675 g) potatoes
1 tblsp (15 ml) fresh chopped parsley

Oven temperature 350°F, 180°C, Gas Mark 4
Cut the lamb into cubes, heat the oil in a frying pan and cook the lamb for 5 to 7 minutes until brown all over. Stir

in the flour, add the stock and cider and stir until the liquid thickens. Stir in the tomato purée, rosemary and plenty of salt and pepper. Transfer the mixture to a large ovenproof dish and rinse out the frying pan.

Peel the parsnip and cut it into 2 in (5 cm) strips. Peel and slice the onion, garlic and turnip, and peel, core and slice the apples.

Melt 1 oz (25g) of the butter in the frying pan, and lightly toss the vegetables in the butter to coat; remove the vegetables with a slotted spoon and combine them with the lamb.

Peel and slice the potatoes thinly to $\frac{1}{4}$ in ($\frac{1}{2}$ cm) thick. Melt the remaining 1 oz (25g) of butter in the pan, toss the potatoes in the butter and spread them over the lamb and vegetables.

Cover the dish with foil, make a few small holes for the steam to escape and cook in the preheated oven for 1 hour 15 minutes. Raise the temperature to 375°F, 190°C, Gas Mark 5, remove the foil and cook a further 45 minutes until the potatoes are golden brown.

Sprinkle with parsley and serve piping hot.

PORK AND VEAL

SWEET AND SOUR CHINESE RIBS
serves 4

The secret ingredient in this recipe which makes these ribs taste so authentic is the five-spice powder. The five spices are star anise, anise pepper, fennel, cloves and cinnamon and you can buy it ready mixed from most supermarkets nowadays. Don't be tempted to use more than is suggested because it is very fragrant. Save any leftover sauce and store it in the refrigerator for up to a week to spread over hamburgers or grilled meat.

1 lb (450 g) cooking apples
¼ pt (125 ml) freshly squeezed orange juice
¼ pt (125 ml) dark malt vinegar
¼ pt (125 ml) water
3 tblsp (45 ml) soy sauce
5 tblsp (75 ml) demerara sugar
½ tsp (2.5 ml) five-spice powder
2½ lbs (1.1 kg) lean pork spare ribs

Oven temperature 350°F, 180°C, Gas Mark 4
Peel, core and slice the apples into a pan. Add the orange juice, vinegar, water, soy sauce, sugar and five-spice powder and stir well. Bring the mixture to the boil, reduce the heat and simmer for 10 to 12 minutes or until the apples are soft. Whisk the mixture to make a thick dark purée. Place the spare ribs in a large shallow ovenproof dish and pour the sauce over them. Cover with foil and cook in the centre of the preheated oven for 2 hours. Remove the foil and cook the ribs for a further hour or until the ribs are crispy and the sauce has thickened. The meat should feel tender. Remove the ribs from the sauce and serve with a green salad or some plain boiled rice. Best eaten with the fingers!

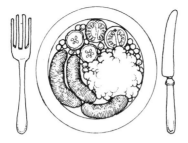

HOME-MADE SAUSAGES WITH GRATED APPLE AND HERBS
serves 4

Grated apples give these little sausages a light fresh taste. Serve them crisply grilled with fluffy creamed potatoes and a salad.

1 lb (450 g) minced pork
8 oz (225 g) minced veal
1 tblsp (15 ml) fresh chopped sage
pinch of dried marjoram
1 oz (25 g) fresh breadcrumbs
1 tsp (5 ml) salt
1 tsp (5 ml) freshly ground black pepper
3 sweet eating apples
flour to coat

Place the pork, veal, sage, marjoram, breadcrumbs, salt and pepper in a bowl. Peel, core and finely grate the apples and add them to the bowl. Mix all the ingredients together thoroughly.

Sprinkle a little flour onto a working surface. Spoon out even-sized balls of the mixture and roll them in the flour to make chunky sausage shapes.

Grill for 8 to 10 minutes until evenly browned.

PORK TENDERLOIN STUFFED WITH SPINACH AND APPLE
serves 4

The tenderloins can be filled with the apple and spinach stuffing in advance, leaving little last-minute work to be done.

Stuffing
8 oz (225 g) fresh spinach
2 small sweet eating apples
1 oz (25 g) butter
1 tsp (5 ml) flour
1 egg yolk
salt and freshly ground black pepper

2 pork tenderloins each weighing 12 oz (350 g)
oil
4 fl oz (100 ml) dry cider or wine
knob of butter

Oven temperature 325°F, 170°C, Gas Mark 3

To make the stuffing: wash the spinach and remove the stalks. Peel, core and slice the apples. Place the spinach and apples in a pan with a little water, cover and simmer for 10 minutes until both are tender. Drain and chop the spinach and apples together on a board.

Melt the butter in a pan, add the spinach and apples and cook over a medium heat, stirring continuously, until all the liquid has evaporated and the mixture begins to stick to the pan.

Stir in the flour, cook a moment or two longer, still stirring, and remove from the heat. Beat the egg yolk and stir it into the mixture, with salt and pepper. Set aside.

Slit the tenderloins lengthways down one side through to approximately ¾ in (2 cm) of the other side. Open them out flat, cover with a piece of foil and beat with a meat mallet. Remove the foil and spoon half the stuffing down the middle of each. Sew up each tenderloin with fine string leaving a short piece of string at each end.

Heat a little oil in an ovenproof dish just large enough to hold the meat. Roll the meat in the oil until it begins to turn colour. Sprinkle with salt and pepper. Cover loosely with foil and cook for 45 minutes in the preheated oven.

Raise the heat to 400°F, 200°C, Gas Mark 6. Remove the foil and cook a further 15 minutes until brown. Remove the meat and keep warm. Deglaze the pan juices with the cider or wine, let it bubble over a fairly high heat until it thickens slightly, then stir in the butter.

Carefully pull the string away from the pork, cut into neat slices and arrange on plates with a little sauce poured over.

PORK, APPLE AND CHESTNUT PIE
WITH SHERRY
serves 4

This excellent and economical pie is perfect for picnics and has an easy to make pastry and a distinctly autumnal filling. Serve it hot with plenty of gravy and Brussels sprouts, or cold with a red cabbage salad.

Pastry
9 oz (275 g) plain flour
1 tsp (5 ml) salt
3 oz (90 g) lard
$\frac{1}{4}$ pt (150 ml) water
1 beaten egg to glaze

Filling
8 oz (225 g) fresh chestnuts
8 oz (225 g) sweet eating apples
8 oz (225 g) lean minced pork
6 tblsp (90 ml) dry sherry
1 tsp (5 ml) salt
$\frac{1}{2}$ tsp (2.5 ml) freshly ground black pepper
1 egg

Oven temperature 400°F, 200°C, Gas Mark 6
To make the pastry: sieve the flour and salt into a bowl. Melt the lard in the water in a small pan and bring to the boil. Add to the flour and mix with a fork to form a soft dough. Lightly flour the work surface and knead the dough lightly until it is smooth and glossy. Roll out $\frac{2}{3}$ of the pastry to a 10 in (25 cm) round and use to line an 8 in (20 cm) round deep loose-bottomed cake tin. Roll the remaining pastry out to an 8 in (20 cm) round and set aside.

To make the filling: cut around the middle of the chestnuts with a sharp knife. Grill for 5 minutes or until the skins blacken and split. Remove the hard outer shell and the furry insides holding each nut with a teatowel. Chop the nuts roughly. Peel, core and finely chop the apples. Place the chestnuts, apples and pork in a bowl with the sherry, salt, pepper and egg and mix well together. Spoon the filling into the pastry case, pressing the mixture down well into the corners. Fold the pastry down over the filling to form a lip. Brush with beaten egg. Arrange the pastry lid over the top of the filling and press it down lightly to seal. Brush the top liberally with the beaten egg and make a hole in the centre for the steam to escape.

Cook in the top of the preheated oven for 1 hour 15 minutes to 1 hour 30 minutes or until the pastry is golden. Allow the pie to cool for 5 minutes, then run a knife around the edge of the tin to loosen the side.

RAISED PORK AND APPLE PIE WITH CREAM CHEESE AND GARLIC
serves 8

A loose-bottomed, spring-clip tin will make this pie easier to turn out. The cream cheese melts through the apple layer and keeps the pie moist. It's equally good hot or cold and slices well.

Pastry
12 oz (350 g) plain wholemeal flour
$\frac{1}{2}$ tsp (2.5 ml) salt
3 oz (75 g) lard
3 oz (75 g) margarine
6 tblsp (90 ml) water

Filling
1 lb (450 g) lean pork shoulder steak
4 oz (100 g) smoked streaky bacon
4 oz (100 g) good pork sausagemeat
$\frac{1}{2}$ tsp (2.5 ml) salt
freshly ground black pepper
1 tsp (5 ml) fresh chopped sage
2 tart eating apples
1 small onion
$3\frac{1}{2}$ oz (100 g) pkt cream cheese with garlic
and herbs
1 beaten egg, to glaze

Oven temperature 375°F, 190°C, Gas Mark 5
To make the pastry: place the flour and salt into a bowl. Add the lard and the margarine cut up into small pieces and rub in with the fingertips until the mixture resembles breadcrumbs. Add the water and mix lightly to form a firm dough.

70

Grease an 8 in (20 cm) round deep cake tin and line the base with greaseproof paper.

To make the filling: trim any excess fat from the pork; remove the rind and any bone from the bacon. Mince the pork and bacon with the sausagemeat, salt, pepper and sage. Peel, core and coarsely grate the apples and peel and coarsely grate the onion. Press the grated apple and onion lightly in a sieve to drain off the excess liquid.

Roll out $\frac{2}{3}$ of pastry to a 13 in (33 cm) round. Use to line the base and sides of the tin. Press half the pork mixture into the tin, arrange the apple and onion on top, season with salt and pepper and dot with the cream cheese. Cover with the remaining pork mixture and smooth the top level with the back of a spoon. Fold the pastry sides down over the filling to form a lip and brush with the beaten egg. Roll the remaining pastry out to an 8 in (20 cm) round $\frac{1}{4}$ in ($\frac{1}{2}$ cm) thick and use to cover the filling. Press the edges lightly to seal and mark on a pattern with the back of a spoon. Roll out the trimmings and use to decorate the top. Brush the pie liberally with the egg.

Cook in the centre of the preheated oven for 1 hour 45 minutes. After 30 minutes, lay a double sheet of greaseproof paper over the top to prevent the pastry overbrowning.

PORK AND APPLE PIE WITH PUFF PASTRY
serves 4 to 6

Apples combined with minced pork make a simple, economical and delicious pie.

13 oz (368 g) packet puff pastry
1 egg
2 small sweet eating apples
1 lb (450 g) minced pork
1 finely chopped sage leaf
1 tblsp (15 ml) fresh chopped parsley
salt and freshly ground black pepper

Oven temperature 400°F, 200°C, Gas Mark 6
Butter a 9 in (23 cm) pie plate. Divide the pastry in two, roll out one half and line the plate. Separate the egg and paint the pastry surface with the white. Peel and coarsely grate the apples into a bowl and add the pork, sage, parsley, salt and pepper. Mix well together and spread the meat mixture on top of the pastry, leaving about ½ in (1 cm) clear round the outside. Brush this rim with egg yolk beaten with a little water. Roll out the remaining pastry to a large circle and cover the meat. Trim the edges and press together well to make sure that the two halves are sealed. Prick all over with a fork and brush the top with the reserved egg yolk to glaze.

Bake in the top of the preheated oven for 15 minutes, then reduce the temperature to 375°F, 190°C, Gas Mark 5, and cook a further 30 minutes until the pastry is well risen and golden brown. Serve hot.

POULTRY AND GAME

CHICKEN PARCELS STUFFED WITH
STILTON, CELERY AND APPLE
serves 4

The stuffing tastes equally good in pork fillet or turkey and makes a good topping for hamburgers or lamb burgers too. You can prepare the recipe in advance and keep the chicken parcels covered in the refrigerator for up to a day before you need them.

4 boned chicken breasts
salt and freshly ground black pepper

Stuffing
1 medium-sized sweet eating apple
2 sticks celery
4 oz (125 g) Stilton cheese

1 egg
2 oz (50 g) fresh wholemeal breadcrumbs
oil for frying

Slit each chicken breast lengthways through to $\frac{1}{2}$ in (1 cm) of the edge and open it out. Place each piece between two sheets of greaseproof paper and beat flat with a rolling pin. Season well with salt and pepper.

To make the stuffing: peel and finely chop the apple and wash and finely chop the celery. Cut the rind off the Stilton and crumble the cheese into a bowl. Add the chopped apple and celery and mix well.

Divide the mixture between the flattened chicken breasts and fold over to make a parcel. Beat the edges of the chicken together to seal in the filling.

Lightly beat the egg in a flat dish or soup bowl and dip each parcel in the egg to coat. Cover with breadcrumbs and press the crumbs on gently to cover.

Heat some oil in a large frying pan and cook the parcels over a medium heat for 5 minutes on each side or until the coating is crisp and golden.

TURKEY WITH GINGER AND DRUNKEN APPLES
serves 4

If you have a wok this recipe is easier to do but a large frying pan suffices. It can be prepared the day before and cooked quickly at the last minute. A dash of sesame oil when frying improves the flavour.

> 2 tblsp (30 ml) soy sauce
> 4 tblsp (60 ml) dry cider
> 4 tblsp (60 ml) dry sherry
> 1 tsp (5 ml) dark brown sugar
> 1 lb (450 g) turkey fillet
> 3 slices fresh ginger root
> 1 clove of garlic
> 2 sweet eating apples
> 8 oz (225 g) broccoli
> 2 tblsp (30 ml) oil

Measure the soy sauce, cider, sherry and sugar into a flat-based bowl. Slice the turkey fillet into thin strips. Peel the root ginger and cut it into fine strips; peel and finely slice the garlic. Peel, core and slice the apples.

Add the turkey fillet, ginger, garlic and apples to the soy sauce mixture and toss well to coat. Cover the bowl with cling film and allow to stand in the refrigerator for at least 2 hours or overnight.

Cut the broccoli into tiny florets. Heat the oil in a large frying pan and fry the turkey strips quickly for 2 to 3 minutes. Add the apple slices and broccoli and cook for a further 3 to 4 minutes until warmed through but the broccoli is still crisp. Add some of the juices from the marinade and toss the ingredients well to coat. Serve immediately with plain boiled rice.

APPLE STUFFED DUCKLING WITH MUSHROOM AND RED WINE SAUCE
serves 4

Prepare the stuffing early to allow time for the rum to flavour the apples.

5 lb (2.3 kg) duckling with its liver

Stuffing
3 sweet eating apples
2 oz (50 g) butter
2 tblsp (30 ml) rum
3 oz (75 g) breadcrumbs
1 tsp (5 ml) grated lemon rind
pinch of rubbed sage
1 tblsp (15 ml) fresh chopped parsley
salt and freshly ground black pepper

Sauce
2 oz (50 g) fresh button mushrooms
2 shallots
6 tblsp (90 ml) chicken stock
2 tblsp (30 ml) red wine

Oven temperature 400°F, 200°C, Gas Mark 6

To make the stuffing: peel, core and thinly slice the apples, gently fry them in the butter over a medium heat for 5 minutes until they have softened but not browned. Place in a large bowl, stir in the rum and leave for an hour. Chop the liver from the duckling and add with the breadcrumbs, grated lemon rind, sage, parsley, salt and pepper to make a stiff mixture.

Stuff the duckling with the mixture and prick it all over with a fork. Lightly oil a roasting pan just large enough to take the duckling. Cook in the centre of the preheated oven for $1\frac{1}{2}$ hours. Do not baste, but remove the fat at frequent intervals and set aside.

To make the sauce: wash and slice the mushrooms, and peel and chop the shallots. Heat a little of the duckling's fat in a pan and gently fry the mushrooms and shallots for 2 to 3 minutes without browning. Add the stock, simmer for a few minutes and set aside.

Transfer the duckling to a carving dish and keep warm. Deglaze the pan with the red wine and strain it into the mushroom mixture. Heat the mushroom mixture and allow it to bubble until it has reduced and thickened. Carve the duckling, arrange the slices and stuffing on plates and spoon over a little sauce.

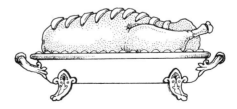

WILD DUCK WITH POACHED APPLES
IN RED WINE SAUCE
serves 4 to 6

Lightly spiced apples poached in red wine are a delicious and attractive accompaniment to wild duck and as all the fiddly work can be done in advance this is a perfect recipe for a dinner party. The following quantities are for 2 ducks which are just right for 4 people but could stretch to 6 if you are a crafty carver!

2 oz (50 g) butter
2 wild ducks
4 shallots
sprig of parsley
salt and freshly ground black pepper
6 sweet eating apples
$\frac{3}{4}$ pt (450 ml) red wine
4 cloves
pinch of cinnamon
butter
1 tsp (5 ml) cornflour

Oven temperature 375°F, 190°C, Gas Mark 5
Melt the butter in an ovenproof dish and lightly brown the ducks all over. Peel the shallots and add to the dish with the parsley, salt and pepper. Cover and cook for 1 hour in the centre of the preheated oven, basting from time to time.

Core the apples, cut in half lengthways and peel. Place the apples in a pan in which they will fit in one layer, add the wine, cloves and cinnamon and simmer uncovered for 10 minutes or until the apples are just tender. Butter an ovenproof dish and arrange the apple halves in one layer. Dot with more butter and set aside. Place the apples in the oven 15 minutes before serving so that they heat through.

Transfer the ducks to a carving dish and keep warm. Strain off the cooking juices into a pan, pressing as much juice from the shallots as possible. Pour in the reserved wine from the apples. Mix the cornflour with a little water and add to the wine, stirring continuously. Allow the sauce to bubble and reduce slightly to thicken.

To serve: remove the wings and legs first, then carve the breast meat into thin slices. Arrange the duck in a fan shape on each plate, surround with apple halves, pour a little sauce over and serve at once.

NORMANDY PHEASANT
serves 3 to 4

Apples and cream are one of the favourite combinations in Normandy cooking and pheasant is an ideal base for this delectable mixture.

2 oz (50 g) butter
1 large pheasant
salt and freshly ground black pepper
4 sweet eating apples
5 tblsp (75 ml) dry cider
$\frac{1}{4}$ pt (142 ml) carton fresh double cream

Oven temperature 375°F, 190°C, Gas Mark 5
Melt 1 oz (25 g) of the butter in a heavy casserole. Brown the pheasant all over in the butter, season with salt and pepper and place uncovered in the oven.

Peel, core and slice the apples. Melt the remaining 1 oz (25 g) of butter in a frying pan and gently toss the apple slices in the melted butter and add with the cider to the casserole. Cook uncovered for 30 minutes. Baste the pheasant with the cider juices, cover and return to the oven for a further 20 minutes.

Transfer the pheasant to a warm serving dish. The cider-apple sauce should be quite thick. Add the cream and stir over high heat until blended and thickened.

Carve the pheasant and serve with the sauce poured over.

ROAST PHEASANT WITH OATMEAL, APPLE AND BACON STUFFING
serves 4

This is a lovely way to cook pheasant; the apples absorb the rich buttery juices and help to keep the bird moist. Steam any extra stuffing in a bowl for 1 hour and serve it separately.

1 pheasant
2 oz (50 g) butter
salt and freshly ground black pepper
1 lb (450 g) sweet eating apples

Stuffing
1 medium-sized onion
1 sweet eating apple
4 oz (125 g) smoked streaky bacon
6 oz (175 g) medium oatmeal
3 oz (75 g) shredded suet
$\frac{1}{2}$ tsp (2.5 ml) salt

Oven temperature 425°F, 220°C, Gas Mark 7
Rinse the pheasant inside and out and pat it dry with kitchen paper. Spread the breast and legs generously with the butter and season well with salt and pepper.

Peel and thickly slice the apples and arrange the slices thickly in the bottom of a small, lightly buttered oven-proof casserole.

To make the stuffing: peel and finely chop the onion; peel, core and finely chop the apple; remove the rind and any bone from the bacon and cut it into small pieces. Place the onion, apple, bacon, oatmeal, suet, salt and pepper in a small bowl and mix well together.

Spoon the stuffing inside the pheasant. Place the

pheasant on the apple slices, cover and cook in the top of the preheated oven for 10 minutes. Reduce the heat to 350°F, 180°C, Gas Mark 4 and cook for a further 45 minutes. Uncover and cook for a further 10 minutes to brown the skin.

Place the pheasant on a warmed serving dish. Stir apples and pheasant juices to a purée and serve separately.

GUINEA FOWL WITH APPLES AND CREAM
serves 4

In this delicious Normandy recipe the guinea fowl is cooked on a bed of apples and surrounded with quartered apples which take on a beautiful golden colour.

2 lb (900 g) firm sweet eating apples
2 oz (50 g) butter
1 guinea fowl
salt and freshly ground black pepper
1 tblsp (15 ml) brandy or calvados
4 fl oz (100 ml) fresh double cream

Oven temperature 350°F, 180°C, Gas Mark 4
Peel, core and slice all but four of the apples. Melt 1 oz (25 g) of the butter in a frying pan and cook the apples over a low heat for about 10 minutes until they have softened. Mash them into a purée with a wooden spoon.

Melt the remaining 1 oz (25 g) of butter in a small ovenproof casserole. Gently turn the guinea fowl in the butter over a medium heat until it is golden brown all over. Remove the guinea fowl from the casserole, place the puréed apples in the base, sprinkle with salt and pepper and place the guinea fowl on top of the apples.

Peel, core and quarter the remaining four apples and

arrange them around the guinea fowl. Sprinkle with brandy or calvados and a little more salt and pepper.

Cover and cook in the preheated oven for 50 minutes.

Carefully remove the guinea fowl and quartered apples and keep warm. Pour the cream into the apple purée and heat through.

Serve the guinea fowl cut into pieces beside the creamy apple purée with the apple quarters arranged on top.

CASSEROLE OF PARTRIDGE WITH
APPLES AND CABBAGE
serves 4

Partridges, not quite young enough to roast, are excellent cooked this way. A few boiled or sautéed potatoes are all that is needed to accompany this dish.

$1\frac{1}{2}$ **lb (675 g) cabbage**
6 cloves of garlic
4 partridges
4 oz (100 g) butter
salt and freshly ground black pepper
1 tblsp (15 ml) fresh chopped parsley
1 tsp (5 ml) paprika
2 medium-sized onions
4 rashers green streaky bacon
6 tblsp (90 ml) dry white wine or cider
4 slightly tart eating apples

Oven temperature 325°F, 170°C, Gas Mark 3
Cut the cabbage into quarters; remove the outside leaves and white core and blanch in boiling salted water for 5 minutes. Drain and set aside. Peel the garlic.

Mix 1 oz (25 g) of the butter with a little salt, pepper, parsley and half the paprika and place a quarter of this mixture and one clove of garlic inside each partridge.

Melt a further 2 oz (50 g) of butter in an ovenproof casserole and gently cook the partridges until they are golden brown all over. Transfer them to a plate.

Peel and slice the onions and slice the remaining 2 cloves of garlic. Cut the bacon into small dice. Add the onion, garlic and bacon to the casserole and cook over a medium heat for 5 to 7 minutes until lightly browned.

Spread half the onion mixture on the bottom of the

casserole. Arrange half the cabbage on top, cover with the partridges, sprinkle with salt and remaining paprika. Cover with the reserved onion mixture and the remainder of the cabbage. Pour in the wine or cider, dot with the remaining 1 oz (25 g) of butter, cover and simmer over a low heat for 30 minutes.

Peel, core and quarter the apples, add to the casserole and cook in the preheated oven for a further hour. Serve the partridges surrounded by the vegetables. Reduce the sauce over high heat for a minute or two to thicken and pour over.

CHICKEN LIVERS WITH MUSHROOMS, BACON AND APPLES IN A PEPPERED CIDER SAUCE
serves 4

Chicken livers offer remarkable value and have the added bonus of being quick to cook. This recipe makes an ideal supper dish served with plain boiled rice or tagliatelle. The livers are best lightly cooked and just pink in the centre.

8 oz (225 g) streaky bacon
8 oz (225 g) mushrooms
1 lb (450 g) chicken livers
2 sweet eating apples
1 oz (25 g) butter
2 tblsp (30 ml) oil
1 tsp (5 ml) dried green peppercorns or 2 tsp
(10 ml) green peppercorns in brine, drained
salt and freshly ground black pepper
$\frac{1}{4}$ pt (150 ml) dry cider
$\frac{1}{4}$ pt (142 ml) carton fresh single cream

Remove any rind and bone from the bacon and cut into small pieces. Cook in a large frying pan over a medium heat for 5 to 7 minutes with no extra fat until crispy and golden. Wash and slice the mushrooms and rinse the chicken livers. Add to the pan and cook for a further 5 minutes. Peel, core and dice the apples and add with the butter, oil and peppercorns and cook for a further 2 to 3 minutes to soften the apples and warm through. Season with salt and plenty of pepper, add the cider and bring to the boil. Add the cream and heat through, stirring. Check seasoning and serve hot.

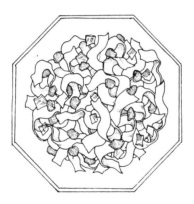

SAUCES

APPLE AND ORANGE SAUCE

A delicious variant of the traditional apple sauce to accompany roast pork.

1 lb (450 g) tart eating apples
1 oz (25 g) butter
1 orange
2 tsp (10 ml) soft brown sugar

Peel, core and grate the apples. Melt the butter in a pan and stir in the apples. Very finely grate the orange rind and squeeze the juice. Add the rind to the apples and cook gently, stirring frequently, for 5 to 10 minutes until the apples are soft. Add the orange juice and sugar to taste and cook until all the liquid has evaporated and the sauce has thickened. Serve hot.

APPLE, CRANBERRY AND ORANGE SAUCE

A colourful and slightly sharp tasting sauce which goes beautifully with lamb and pork.

1 lb (450 g) sweet eating apples
4 oz (125 g) cranberries
1 orange
1 to 2 tblsp (15 to 30 ml) sugar

Peel, core and slice the apples into a pan. Add the cranberries, cover and simmer for 5 to 10 minutes until the fruit is soft. (If necessary add a little water to prevent the fruit sticking to the pan.) Mash the fruit well with the back of a wooden spoon.

Finely grate the orange rind, squeeze the juice and add to the sauce. Stir in the sugar, a spoonful at a time, taking care not to oversweeten the sauce. Cook for 1 to 2 minutes so that the flavours mingle, and serve hot.

APPLE AND CIDER SAUCE

This one is particularly good spread over pork chops. The following quantity will cover four chops nicely.

1 small onion
1 oz (25 g) butter
2 small sweet eating apples
1 tblsp (15 ml) flour
$\frac{1}{4}$ pt (150 ml) dry cider
salt and freshly ground black pepper

Peel and very finely chop the onion. Melt the butter in a pan and cook the onions over a medium heat for 5 minutes until softened but not browned. Peel, core and grate the apples. Stir them into the onions and cook for a few minutes longer. Stir in the flour, and add the cider, salt and pepper. Stir until the sauce has thickened and simmer for 15 minutes, stirring occasionally.

LIGHTLY CURRIED APPLE AND
APRICOT MAYONNAISE

This makes a large quantity of sauce but it can be made in advance and stored in the refrigerator for up to 10 days. Use it to coat cold roast lamb, pork, chicken or leftover Christmas turkey.

1 large onion
2 oz (50 g) butter
2 large cooking apples
2 tblsp (30 ml) vindaloo curry paste
14.8 oz (420 g) can of apricot halves
salt and freshly ground black pepper
$\frac{1}{2}$ pt (300 ml) beef or chicken stock
1 lb (454 g) jar mayonnaise

Peel and finely slice the onion. Melt the butter in a pan, add the onion and fry over a medium heat for 7 to 10 minutes until golden brown. Peel, core and slice the apples into the pan. Add the curry paste and the apples and cook for a further 5 minutes, stirring continuously. Add the apricot halves and their juice and the stock and cook for a further 5 minutes until the apples are soft. Press the mixture through a sieve. Add salt and pepper and allow to cool. Beat the mayonnaise until smooth and stir into the purée. Fold in the cold meat and chill before serving.

PEANUT, CHILLI AND APPLE SAUCE

This thick chilli sauce goes equally well with kebabs of beef, chicken, lamb, pork and fish. It will keep for up to 1 week covered in the refrigerator and up to 1 month in the freezer.

1 large onion
1 large clove of garlic
1 tblsp (15 ml) oil
2 sweet eating apples
1 tblsp (15 ml) lemon juice
$1\frac{1}{2}$ tsp (7.5 ml) chilli powder
$\frac{1}{2}$ tsp (2.5 ml) salt
$\frac{1}{4}$ pt (150 ml) chicken stock
4 tblsp (60 ml) crunchy peanut butter
freshly ground black pepper

Peel and finely chop the onion and garlic. Heat the oil in a small pan and cook the onion and garlic over a medium heat for 7 to 8 minutes until the onion is softened and beginning to brown. Peel, core and slice the apples into the pan. Add the lemon juice, chilli powder, salt, stock, peanut butter and plenty of pepper and simmer for a further 15 minutes stirring occasionally to prevent sticking. Liquidise and return to the heat. Serve hot with the grilled kebabs.

DEVILLED APPLE SAUCE

Serve hot with grilled fish or meat or as a dip for dunking fried chicken pieces in. It will keep well in a screw-top jar for up to 1 week in the refrigerator.

1 medium-sized onion
2 cloves of garlic
1 large tart eating apple
3 oz (75 g) butter
1 tblsp (15 ml) Worcestershire sauce
2 tblsp (30 ml) tomato ketchup
2 tsp (10 ml) made English mustard
1 tsp (5 ml) black treacle
salt and freshly ground black pepper
a few dashes of Tabasco sauce
1 tblsp (15 ml) fresh chopped parsley

Peel and coarsely grate the onion; peel and crush the garlic and peel, core and coarsely grate the apple. Melt the butter in a pan, add the onion, garlic and apple and cook over a medium heat for 2 to 3 minutes only. Add the Worcestershire sauce, tomato ketchup, mustard, treacle, salt and pepper, and bring the mixture to the boil, stirring continuously to prevent the mixture sticking. Boil for a minute, add the Tabasco and parsley and stir well to mix. Serve hot.

SPINACH, APPLE AND CREAM SAUCE

A delicately flavoured sauce which can transform simple chicken breasts or plainly grilled fish into a feast. It can be made in advance and reheated just before serving.

8 oz (225 g) spinach
1 tart eating apple
1 shallot
1 oz (25 g) butter
$\frac{1}{4}$ pt (142 ml) carton fresh double cream
salt and freshly ground black pepper

Remove the spinach stalks, wash the leaves thoroughly and simmer for 7 minutes in a little salted water. Drain well. Peel, core and chop the apple and peel and chop the shallot. Melt the butter in a small frying pan and cook the apples and shallot over a low heat for about 10 minutes until they are soft.

Place the spinach, apples and shallot in the liquidiser with the cream, salt and pepper. Liquidise until smooth. Serve hot.

TARTARE APPLE SAUCE

A creamy but tart sauce which is excellent with fish especially the Deep-Fried Monkfish in Apple Batter on page 41. It will keep well in a jar in the refrigerator for up to 2 weeks.

1 oz (25 g) gherkins
1 oz (25 g) capers
1 oz (25 g) stoned black olives
1 oz (25 g) stoned green olives
1 tblsp (15 ml) finely chopped parsley
$\frac{1}{4}$ pt (150 ml) mayonnaise
$\frac{1}{4}$ pt (150 ml) unsweetened apple purée (made
from 1 large tart eating apple)
salt and freshly ground black pepper

Coarsely chop the gherkins, capers, black and green olives. Place the gherkins, capers, olives and parsley in a bowl with the mayonnaise, the apple purée, salt and pepper and stir well to mix.

PIES AND TARTS

APPLE AND APRICOT PIE WITH CRUMBLY OATMEAL PASTRY
serves 6

Apples and apricots go beautifully together and give the pie a warm, golden filling. The pastry is short and crumbly and really does melt in the mouth. Serve with lots of cream sweetened with honey.

Pastry
3 oz (75 g) plain flour
1 oz (25 g) medium oatmeal
pinch of salt
2 oz (50 g) butter
1 egg yolk
1 tblsp (15 ml) water
oatmeal for rolling

Filling
1 lb (450 g) sweet eating apples
8 oz (225 g) fresh apricots
2 tblsp (30 ml) soft brown sugar
1 tblsp (15 ml) lemon juice

Oven temperature 400°F, 200°C, Gas Mark 6
To make the pastry: sieve the flour into a bowl, add the oatmeal, salt and the butter, cut into small pieces, and rub in with the fingertips until the mixture resembles coarse breadcrumbs. Whisk the egg yolk and the water together and add, stirring well to make a firm dough.

To make the filling: peel, core and quarter the apples, halve the apricots and remove the stones. Layer the apples and apricots in a 2 pt (1.1 l) pie dish and sprinkle each layer with sugar and lemon juice. Lightly dust the work surface with oatmeal and roll the pastry out to about $\frac{1}{4}$ in ($\frac{1}{2}$ cm) thick to an oval larger than the pie dish. Cut a strip from round the edge of the pastry, arrange it on the lip of the pie dish and brush with water.

Cover the pie with the pastry and press the edges well to seal. Trim off the excess and knock up the edges with the back of a knife. Flute the edges and use the pastry trimmings to decorate the top of the pie.

Bake in the top of the preheated oven for 30 minutes or until the pastry is golden. Serve hot.

CHEESE AND APPLE PIE
serves 6 to 8

They say that an apple without cheese is like a kiss without a squeeze and this recipe proves that they certainly go extremely well together. Use any of the traditional English cheeses in the pastry but a well coloured Cheddar or Red Leicester gives the pastry a terrific glow. The apples are tossed in a buttery lemon toffee before cooking.

Pastry
6 oz (175 g) plain flour
pinch of salt
pinch of dry mustard powder
4 oz (125 g) butter
4 oz (125 g) Red Leicester cheese
1 egg yolk
1 tblsp (15 ml) water
beaten egg to glaze

Filling
1 medium-sized lemon
2 oz (50 g) unsalted butter
2 oz (50 g) dark soft brown sugar
2 lb (900 g) sweet eating apples

Oven temperature 400°F, 200°C, Gas Mark 6
To make the pastry: sieve the flour, salt and mustard powder in a bowl. Coarsely grate in the butter, scooping some flour on to the grater from time to time to stop the butter sticking, and finely grate in the cheese. Stir lightly to mix. Lightly whisk the egg yolk and the water together and add, stirring well to make a firm dough.

To make the filling: finely grate the lemon rind and

95

squeeze the juice. Melt the butter in a large pan; add the sugar, lemon rind and juice and shake the pan over a medium heat to make a soft toffee. Do not stir or the sugar will crystallise. Peel, core and slice the apples into the pan and toss lightly to coat. Pour into a 3 pt (1.7 l) pie dish.

Lightly flour the work surface and roll out the pastry to an oval larger than the pie dish about $\frac{1}{4}$ in ($\frac{1}{2}$ cm) thick. Cut a strip from round the edge of the pastry and press it onto the lip of the pie dish. Brush with beaten egg. Arrange the pastry over the top of the filling and press the edges well to seal. Trim off the excess pastry and knock up the edge with the back of a knife. Mark on a pattern with a fork, flute the edge and brush the pastry well with beaten egg.

Cook in the top of the preheated oven for 25 to 30 minutes or until the pastry is golden brown. Serve hot.

APPLE AND GREENGAGE TART
serves 4

Greengages are particularly good in this apple tart but plums could be used instead.

shortcrust pastry made with
4 oz (125 g) flour
$\frac{1}{2}$ pt (300 ml) apple purée made from 1 lb (450 g)
sweet eating apples
8 oz (225 g) greengages
1 oz (25 g) demerara sugar

Oven temperature 375°F, 190°C, Gas Mark 5
Butter an 8 in (20 cm) flan tin; roll out the pastry and line the tin. Spoon the apple purée on to the pastry, smoothing the surface with the back of the spoon.

Slice the greengages in half, remove the stones and

arrange them on the apple purée — they should not quite touch each other — and press them into the purée. Sprinkle with the demerara sugar and bake in the top of the preheated oven for 40 minutes or until the pastry is golden and begins to shrink from the side of the tin.

CREAMY APPLE TART
serves 6

There are many recipes for apple tarts with creamy fillings. This one is particularly good. The filling might appear a little meagre before baking but it puffs up and spreads during cooking.

> **3 large sweet eating apples**
> **4 tblsp (60 ml) sugar**
> **$\frac{1}{2}$ tsp (2.5 ml) cinnamon**
> **shortcrust pastry made from**
> **6 oz (175 g) flour**
> **2 egg yolks**
> **$\frac{1}{4}$ pt (142 ml) carton fresh soured cream**

Oven temperature 400°F, 200°C, Gas Mark 6
Peel, core and slice the apples and roll them in 2 tblsp (30 ml) of sugar mixed with the cinnamon. Butter a 9 in (23 cm) flan tin; roll out the pastry and line the tin. Arrange the apple slices on the pastry. Bake in the top of the preheated oven for 25 minutes.

Beat the egg yolks, then gradually beat in the soured cream and the remaining 2 tblsp (30 ml) sugar. Pour the mixture over the centre of the apples and smooth it outwards.

Bake for a further 20 to 25 minutes until the tart is golden and the filling is set. Serve warm rather than hot.

APPLE AND ALMOND TART
serves 8 to 10

This is an exceptionally attractive tart. It can be made in advance and warmed through in the oven just before serving.

**shortcrust pastry made with
8 oz (225 g) flour**

Almond filling
**4 oz (100 g) butter
4 oz (100 g) caster sugar
1 egg plus 1 yolk
1 tblsp (15 ml) brandy or calvados
4 oz (100 g) ground almonds
1 oz (25 g) flour**

**4 small sweet eating apples
3 tblsp (45 ml) apple jelly or
strained apricot jam**

Oven temperature 375°F, 190°C, Gas Mark 5
Butter a 10 in (25 cm) flan tin; roll out the pastry, line the tin and set aside.

To make the filling: beat the butter and sugar until the mixture is light and creamy, beat in the egg and the egg yolk, add the brandy or calvados, stir in the ground almonds and finally the flour. Pour into the prepared pastry case.

Peel the apples, cut them in half and scoop out the cores with the tip of a teaspoon. Cut each half apple into thin slices crosswise, keeping the slices firmly together. Place one sliced half in the centre of the tart and the others round the outside to resemble the spokes of a wheel. Press the halves down gently, at the same time very slightly tilting the outside halves towards the edge of the dish. Bake for 35 to 40 minutes in the centre of the preheated oven until the pastry is cooked, the apples are tender and the almond filling set.

Shortly before serving melt the apple jelly or apricot jam slowly in a small, heavy saucepan and brush over the tart. Serve the tart warm rather than cold or hot.

TARTE TATIN
(UPSIDE DOWN APPLE TART)
serves 4 to 6

This tart needs to cook longer than others. When the tart is turned over the pastry makes a crisp bed for the caramelised apples. It is delicious!

1 oz (25 g) butter
4 oz (100 g) sugar
5 large sweet eating apples
sweet shortcrust pastry made with
4 oz (100 g) flour

Oven temperature 375°F, 190°C, Gas Mark 5
Melt the butter in a shallow 8 in (20 cm) round cake tin; sprinkle on half the sugar. Peel, core and slice the apples, neatly arrange a layer of apples over the sugar and build up the tart with layers of apples and sugar.

Roll out the pastry to an 8 in (20 cm) round, cover the tin and trim the pastry so that it just overlaps the side of the tin but do not press it down. Prick the top. Bake in the centre of the preheated oven for 1 hour (if the pastry is browning too much lower the heat). The tart is cooked when the apple juices thicken and caramelise.

To serve: cover the tart with the serving plate and quickly turn over. You are then left with the pastry underneath; the apples neatly arranged on the top will have turned a lovely pink colour coated in their own caramel.

CARRÉ AUX POMMES
serves 6

The recipe for this delicious pie comes from Normandy.
It appears enormous but is very light and not nearly as
filling as it looks!

2 oz (50 g) raisins
2 tblsp (30 ml) rum, madeira or cognac
1 oz (25 g) blanched almonds
4 firm sweet eating apples
2 oz (50 g) butter
2 oz (50 g) caster sugar
13 oz (368 g) packet puff pastry
1 beaten egg

Oven temperature 400°F, 200°C, Gas Mark 6
Soak the raisins in the rum, madeira or cognac for one
hour. Finely chop the almonds. Peel, core and slice the
apples. Melt the butter in a frying pan and gently cook the
apples over a medium heat for 5 minutes to soften. Add
the raisins and their juice, almonds and sugar, and stir
well.

Divide the pastry into two equal pieces. Roll each piece
into a square and trim to the same size. Place one half on a
buttered baking sheet, spread the apple mixture on to it,
leaving a 1 in (2.5 cm) border all round, and brush with
water. Place the other half on top and press the edges with
a fork to seal. Trim the edge with a sharp knife. Prick the
top with the knife and glaze with the beaten egg. Bake in
the top of the preheated oven for 30 minutes until the pie
is well risen and golden brown.

APPLE STRUDEL
serves 4 to 6

They say, in Vienna, that strudel pastry should be so thin
that you can read a love letter through it! Don't worry,
strudel pastry is nothing like ordinary pastry, it stretches
like elastic and it is not difficult to make.

Strudel pastry
5 oz (150 g) flour
pinch of salt
1 small egg
1 tblsp (15 ml) oil
3 tblsp (45 ml) warm water
flour

Filling
$\frac{1}{2}$ oz (15 g) butter
1 oz (25 g) fresh white breadcrumbs
$1\frac{1}{2}$ lb (675 g) cooking apples
1 oz (25 g) blanched almonds
1 oz (25 g) raisins
1 oz (25 g) sugar

1 oz (25 g) melted butter
icing sugar

Oven temperature 350°F, 180°C, Gas Mark 4

To make the pastry: sieve the flour and salt into a bowl. Beat the egg and pour it into a well in the centre with the oil and water. Work together with a wooden spoon until the dough comes away from the sides of the bowl. Turn the dough out onto a floured work surface and knead for approximately 5 minutes until it is smooth and silky. Sprinkle with flour, cover with a cloth and leave for 30 minutes.

To make the filling: melt the butter in a pan and fry the breadcrumbs until golden brown. Peel, core and slice the apples very finely. Chop the almonds.

Lay a clean tea towel onto a large flat surface and sprinkle it with flour. Pull the dough out a little and place it in the centre. Roll out the dough with a rolling pin, always working from the centre outwards. When the dough is larger than the rolling pin pull it with your hands until it is the size of the towel. (Don't panic if you get the odd tear, it is all going to be rolled up!) Trim the edges.

Sprinkle the breadcrumbs evenly over the pastry, spread the apples on top, scatter over the nuts and raisins and sprinkle with sugar.

Lightly butter a large baking sheet. Pick up one end of the tea towel and lift it slightly so that the strudel begins to roll over on to itself. Then pull the towel higher so that the strudel rolls over and over like a Swiss roll. Roll it straight on to the baking sheet, making sure that the join is underneath. Tuck the ends in neatly to seal.

Bake in the centre of the preheated oven for 25 minutes, brush with melted butter and return to the oven for a further 5 minutes. Carefully lift it out on to a serving dish and sprinkle with sieved icing sugar.

PUDDINGS

RUM AND APPLE PANCAKES
serves 4 to 6

Rum flavoured apples make a delicious filling for pancakes.

Filling
1 lb (450 g) cooking apples
2 oz (50 g) butter
pinch of cinnamon
2 tblsp (30 ml) soft brown sugar
2 tblsp (30 ml) rum or madeira

Pancakes
$\frac{1}{2}$ pt (300 ml) milk and water mixed
1 egg
1 tblsp (15 ml) sugar
pinch of salt
4 oz (125 g) plain flour
oil for frying

To make the filling: peel, core and slice the apples into a pan. Add the butter, cinnamon and brown sugar and cook over a medium heat for 5 to 7 minutes or until the apples are soft. Add the rum or madeira, stir it in quickly and cook a moment or two longer and keep warm.

To make the pancakes: place the milk, water, egg, sugar, salt and flour in a liquidiser and blend until smooth. Make the pancakes, fill each with a few spoonfuls of apple mixture, roll up and serve immediately.

RICH BAKED APPLES
serves 4

Richer and decidedly more elegant than the traditional baked apples.

butter for greasing
4 large sweet eating apples
2 oz (50 g) sugar
3 oz (75 g) butter
$\frac{1}{4}$ pt (150 ml) dry cider
4 slices of bread
2 tblsp (30 ml) apple or redcurrant jelly

Oven temperature 350°F, 180°C, Gas Mark 4
Lightly butter an ovenproof dish just large enough to hold the apples.

Peel the apples and remove the cores. Place the apples in the dish, sprinkle with sugar. Cut 1 oz (25 g) of the butter in four and place a knob of butter inside each apple. Pour in the cider, bring to simmering point on the top of the stove. Bake in the centre of the preheated oven for 20 to 30 minutes until the apples are soft when pierced with a skewer but not in danger of collapse. Carefully lift out the apples with a slotted spoon and set aside.

In the meantime cut the bread into apple-sized rounds with a biscuit cutter. Melt the remaining 2 oz (50 g) butter in a frying pan and fry the bread rounds until golden and crispy. Arrange on serving plates. Stir the jelly into the apple-cider liquid and allow to melt. Reduce over a high heat until the sauce is thick enough to coat the back of a spoon. Place the apples on the bread rounds, pour the sauce over and serve hot.

UPSIDE DOWN APPLE PUDDING
serves 6

A cold weather favourite. Don't be put off by the quantity of flour; it does look stodgy when you make it but emerges from the oven remarkably light.

1 oz (25 g) soft brown sugar
6 oz (175 g) butter
1 medium-sized cooking apple
$\frac{1}{4}$ pt (150 ml) milk
4 oz (100 g) granulated sugar
10 oz (275 g) self-raising flour
1 beaten egg

Oven temperature 350°F, 180°C, Gas Mark 4
Melt the brown sugar and 2 oz (50 g) of the butter in a deep 8 in (20 cm) cake tin. Peel, core and slice the apple thickly and arrange over the sugar and butter and set aside.

Heat the remaining 4 oz (125 g) of butter and the milk together in a pan until the butter is melted. Place the sugar and flour in a bowl, add the milk mixture and the beaten egg and stir well.

Spoon the cake mixture over the apple and level with the back of the spoon and bake in the centre of the pre-heated oven for 50 minutes or until well risen and golden.

APPLE HAT
serves 4

This is a traditional steamed suet pudding that's never been known to be refused! It's tangy, sweet and buttery, very filling, and the perfect pudding on cold winter days.

Pastry
6 oz (175 g) self-raising flour
$\frac{1}{2}$ tsp (2.5 ml) salt
3 oz (75 g) shredded suet
$\frac{1}{4}$ pt (150 ml) cold water

Filling
1 lb (450 g) cooking apples
1 large lemon
2 oz (50 g) dark soft brown sugar
2 oz (50 g) raisins

To make the pastry: sieve the flour and salt into a bowl. Add the suet and stir lightly. Add the water and stir with a knife to make a soft dough. Lightly flour the work surface and knead the dough lightly until smooth and elastic. Cut off a quarter of the pastry and set aside. Roll the remaining pastry into a large round, and use to line a $2\frac{1}{2}$ pt (1.3 l) pudding basin.

To make the filling: peel, core and thinly slice the apples; finely grate the lemon rind and squeeze the juice. Layer the apples in the bowl with the lemon rind, sugar and raisins and 1 tblsp (15 ml) of the lemon juice.

Roll the remaining piece of pastry out to a round to fit the top of the pudding. Roll the top edge of the pastry side down to form an even lip level with the filling. Brush the lip with water, lay the pastry lid over the filling and press the edges lightly to seal. Cover the basin with buttered greaseproof paper and tie with string, leaving enough to form a handle over the top.

Cover and steam for 3 hours, topping up with boiling water from time to time. Run a knife round the side to loosen the pastry and invert the pudding onto the serving plate. Serve immediately.

N.B. If you have a microwave oven the pudding takes just 8 minutes on full power in a 650 watt oven!

LEMON AND APPLE CHEESECAKE
serves 6 to 8

A baked cheesecake is always greeted with murmurs of appreciation at the end of a meal and this one is tangy with lemon and studded with sultanas. It keeps remarkably well, covered with cling film in the refrigerator for up to 10 days. If you are feeling really greedy serve it with fresh double cream!

1 large lemon
2 oz (50 g) sultanas
3 oz (75 g) unsalted butter
4 oz (100g) caster sugar
3 eggs
1 lb (450 g) curd cheese
1 tblsp (15 ml) cornflour
1 lb (450 g) tart eating apples
pinch of salt

Oven temperature 300°F, 150°C, Gas Mark 2
Finely grate the lemon rind and squeeze the juice. Place the rind and the juice in a small bowl with the sultanas and allow to stand for 15 minutes while you make the rest of the filling.

Cream the butter and the sugar together in a bowl until they are light and fluffy. Separate the eggs, add the yolks to the butter mixture and place the whites in a bowl. Beat the egg yolks into the mixture with the curd cheese and cornflour until the mixture is soft and creamy.

Peel, core and finely chop the apples and add them to the cheese mixture with a pinch of salt, the sultanas, lemon rind and juice. Whisk the reserved egg whites until they are stiff but not dry and fold gently into the cheese mixture.

Butter the sides and base of an 8 in (20 cm) round, deep, loose-bottomed cake tin and coat with plain flour. Shake out the excess flour and gently pour in the cheesecake mixture. Bake in the centre of the preheated oven for 1 hr or until the top begins to look shiny and pale golden, the edge feels firm but the centre still feels a little soft. Allow to cool completely before you remove the tin. Transfer the cheesecake to a serving plate and allow to chill before serving.

APPLE AND WINE CREAM
WITH CARDAMOM
serves 8

A simple but successful sweet made of wine-simmered apples flavoured with cardamom. Any leftovers are also delicious served over hot apple pie.

1 lb (450 g) cooking apples
4 green cardamom pods
$\frac{1}{2}$ pt (300 ml) dry white wine
$\frac{1}{2}$ pt (284 ml) carton fresh double cream
2 tblsp (30 ml) Drambuie
1 oz (25 g) light soft brown sugar

Slice the apples into a pan, split open the cardamom pods and add to the pan with the wine. Cover and simmer gently for 10 to 15 minutes or until the apples are soft. Beat to a purée and sieve into a bowl. Cool completely. Pour the cream into a bowl and whisk until it just holds its shape, whisk in the cooked apple purée, the Drambuie and the sugar and divide the mixture between glasses. Serve chilled.

BLACKBERRY AND APPLE TRIFLE
serves 6 to 8

Blackberries and apples make a very good marriage and ring the changes in this popular pudding. It's worth making real custard, but canned or instant can be used if time is short.

1 large cooking apple
8 oz (225 g) fresh blackberries
1 tblsp (15 ml) dark brown sugar

Custard
3 egg yolks
1 oz (25 g) caster sugar
2 tsp (10 ml) cornflour
$\frac{1}{4}$ pt (150 ml) milk
$\frac{1}{4}$ pt (142 ml) carton fresh single cream

8 bought trifle sponges
4 tblsp (60 ml) bramble jelly
$\frac{1}{4}$ pt (150 ml) rose wine or sweet cider
$\frac{1}{4}$ pt (142 ml) carton fresh whipping cream
1 red-skinned apple
bramble leaves to decorate

Peel, core and slice the cooking apple into a small pan. Add the blackberries and the sugar and cook for about 5 minutes only until the apple has softened slightly and the juices begin to run from the blackberries. Cool completely.

To make the custard: place the egg yolks, sugar and cornflour in a large bowl and mix until blended. Pour the milk and the single cream into a pan and bring to just below boiling point. Pour the mixture into the egg yolks, stirring continuously. Return the mixture to the pan and cook over a very low heat for about 5 minutes, stirring well until the mixture thickens slightly. Do not allow the mixture to boil or it will curdle. Remove the pan from the heat and allow it to cool slightly.

Split the trifle sponges and spread them with the bramble jelly. Arrange them in the base of a glass serving dish and soak with the wine or the cider.

Spread the blackberry and apple mixture over the top and pour over the slightly cooled custard. Allow to set. Lightly whisk the whipping cream until it just holds its shape. Spread the cream over the custard and mark on a pattern with the back of the spoon. Cut the red-skinned apple into slices and remove the core. Arrange on cream, decorate with well washed bramble leaves and serve.

HONEY APPLE CHEESECAKE
serves 6 to 8

Not really a cheesecake as only cream is used! It is attractive and deliciously fresh tasting, subtly flavoured with honey. It is easy to make and can be prepared very quickly indeed if you already have a supply of apple purée in the freezer, and, as it can be made a day or two in advance, it is ideal for a party.

Crumb base and topping
6 oz (175 g) digestive biscuits
3 oz (75 g) butter

Filling
$\frac{3}{4}$ pt (400 ml) apple purée made from
$1\frac{1}{2}$ lb (675 g) sweet eating apples
2 tblsp (30 ml) clear honey
$\frac{1}{2}$ oz (15 g) pkt powdered gelatine
$\frac{1}{2}$ pt (284 ml) carton fresh double cream

Lightly butter a $7\frac{1}{2}$ in (19 cm) spring-sided tin and line the sides and bottom with greaseproof paper. Crush the biscuits with a rolling pin. Melt the butter and mix in the biscuits. Set aside 3 tblsp (45 ml) of the mixture and press the rest into the bottom of the prepared tin.

Heat the apple purée in a small pan with the honey and stir until it has dissolved.

Dissolve the gelatine in a little cold water, following the instructions on the packet. Stir it into the apple purée and leave to cool.

Whip the cream until it is stiff enough to hold its shape and carefully fold it into the apples. Pour the mixture onto the prepared biscuit base, scatter the remaining biscuit mixture on the top and leave to set.

To serve: run a knife around the tin, and ease the paper away from the sides of the tin *before* releasing the spring clip. Carefully peel the paper from the sides of the cake. Run a palette knife between the bottom of the cake and the paper and very carefully lift the cake onto a serving plate.

SWEDISH APPLE CHARLOTTE
serves 4

Despite its simplicity this pudding is quite delicious. It is best eaten cold at room temperature rather than straight from the refrigerator.

2 oz (50 g) butter
4 oz (100 g) fresh white breadcrumbs
2 oz (50 g) demerara sugar
$\frac{1}{2}$ pt (300 ml) apple purée (made from
1 lb (450 g) sweet eating apples)

Melt the butter in a large frying pan and fry the bread-crumbs stirring well until the crumbs are golden. (Unless you have a very large frying pan it is easier to do this in two separate batches.) Mix in the demerara sugar.

Spread half the breadcrumb mixture in a small soufflé or straight-sided dish, pour in the apple purée and top with the remaining breadcrumbs.

Serve with fresh cream.

ICE-CREAMS AND SORBETS

APPLE AND CRANBERRY ICE-CREAM
makes 2 pt (1.1 l)

Cranberries and apples combine well in this rich, fruity ice-cream. Save it for the 'grown ups'!

1 lb (450 g) cooking apples
8 oz (225 g) fresh or frozen cranberries
6 oz (175 g) sugar
½ pt (300 ml) water
2 tblsp (30 ml) port
½ pt (284 ml) carton fresh double cream

Peel, core and slice the apples into a pan. Add the cranberries, sugar and water, cover and simmer over a medium heat for 10 to 15 minutes until completely soft. Liquidise or pass through a sieve. Allow to cool.

Add the port and cream. Stir thoroughly and freeze. When the ice-cream is almost frozen, beat it well to break down the ice crystals and continue freezing.

TANGERINE AND APPLE SORBET
makes 2 pt (1.1 l)

Perfect for cleansing the palate between courses at the Christmas lunch. So easy to make but with a very refreshing flavour.

8 tangerines
1 pt (600 ml) apple purée (made from
2 lb (900 g) cooking apples)
2 tblsp (30 ml) lemon juice
4 eggs
orange colouring if desired
4 oz (125 g) caster sugar

Finely grate the rind of the tangerines and squeeze the juice. Place rind and juice in a large bowl with the apple purée and the lemon juice. Separate the eggs and add the yolks to the apple purée and place the whites in a bowl. Mix the apple purée mixture well together and add orange colouring if desired. Whisk the egg whites until they are stiff but not dry and gradually whisk in the sugar to make a stiff shiny meringue. Fold the apple purée into the meringue mixture using a metal spoon and pour the mixture into a large tray. Freeze until hard.

CIDER AND APPLE SORBET
makes $1\frac{1}{2}$ pt (900 ml)

An unusual and very refreshing sorbet in which only good quality cider should be used.

8 oz (225 g) granulated sugar
$\frac{1}{2}$ pt (300 ml) water
2 medium-sized sweet eating apples
$\frac{1}{2}$ pt (300 ml) cider
juice of 1 lemon

Slowly dissolve the sugar in the water over a medium heat. Bring to the boil and boil rapidly for five minutes.

Slice the apples and cook with a little water over a medium heat for 5 to 10 minutes until they are soft. Sieve and add to the sugar syrup. Cool and stir in the cider and lemon juice and freeze. When it has almost frozen, beat it well to break down the ice crystals and continue freezing.

APPLE AND GOOSEBERRY ICE CREAM
makes $1\frac{1}{2}$ pt (900 m l)

Apples add a subtle flavour to what can be an overpower-ingly strong fruit, in this creamy ice.

8 oz (225 g) gooseberries
1 lb (450 g) cooking apples
8 oz (225 g) sugar
$\frac{1}{4}$ pt (150 ml) water
$\frac{1}{2}$ pt (284 ml) carton fresh double cream

Top and tail the gooseberries and place in a pan. Core the

116

apples, do not skin, and slice finely into the pan. Cover and simmer with the water and sugar until very tender. Sieve and leave to cool.

Pour the cream into a bowl and whisk until it just holds its shape. Fold into the purée. Freeze until almost frozen, beat well and return to the freezer.

BLACKBERRY AND APPLE SORBET
makes 2 pt (1.1 l)

This is refreshing and has a vivid colour. It's made by a speedy meringue method and doesn't need beating after freezing.

1 lb (450 g) cooking apples
1 lb (450 g) blackberries
2 tblsp (30 ml) water
4 eggs
8 oz (225 g) caster sugar

Slice the apples into a large pan. Add the blackberries and the water, cover the pan and simmer gently for 15 minutes, shaking the pan occasionally to prevent sticking. Beat to a purée with a wooden spoon and sieve into a bowl. Separate the eggs. Add the yolks to the purée, stir well to mix and allow to cool. Whisk the egg whites until stiff but not dry. Gradually whisk in the sugar, a little at a time to make a stiff shiny meringue. Fold in the cooled apple purée and pour the mixture into a container. Freeze until solid.

APPLE, WHISKY AND MARMALADE ICE-CREAM
makes about 3 pt (1.7 l)

For grown ups only! A rich creamy pudding with a bitter-sweet flavour. Serve in small quantities. Like most ice-creams and sorbets, allow it to thaw slightly in the refrigerator for 30 minutes before serving.

**1 lb (454 g) jar thick-cut traditional
dark marmalade
$\frac{1}{4}$ pt (150 ml) whisky
$\frac{1}{2}$ oz (15 g) powdered gelatine
1 pt (568 ml) carton fresh double cream
1 pt (600 ml) apple purée (made from 2 lb
(900 g) cooking apples)**

Spoon the marmalade into a small pan, add the whisky and heat gently until the marmalade dissolves. Do not boil. Remove the pan from the heat and allow to cool. Measure 4 tblsp (60 ml) of cold water into a small bowl, sprinkle in the gelatine and stand the bowl in a pan of simmering water. Heat for about 5 minutes or until the gelatine dissolves to a clear liquid. Pour the gelatine into the marmalade mixture and stir well to mix.

Pour the cream into a bowl and whisk lightly until it just holds its shape. Fold in the apple purée and the cold marmalade mixture and pour the mixture into a large tray and freeze until hard.

CAKES AND BAKES

CARROT AND APPLE CAKE
WITH CREAM CHEESE FROSTING

This is a superb moist but crumbly cake. Serve it with the frosting and marzipan decoration if you've friends coming for tea, but it's just as tasty without. Store without the frosting, wrapped in foil in an airtight tin for up to 10 days; with frosting for up to 3 days.

Cake
$\frac{1}{4}$ pt (150 ml) corn oil
5 oz (150 g) soft brown sugar
3 eggs
1 tsp (5 ml) vanilla essence
4 oz (100 g) ground almonds
1 small carrot
1 large sweet eating apple
6 oz (175 g) wholemeal flour
1 tsp (5 ml) bicarbonate of soda
1 tsp (5 ml) baking powder
1 tsp (5 ml) cinnamon
1 tsp (5 ml) salt

Frosting
3 oz (75 g) cream cheese
2 oz (50 g) butter
$\frac{1}{2}$ tsp (2.5 ml) vanilla essence
4 oz (100 g) icing sugar

Decoration
4 oz (100 g) white almond paste
red, yellow and green food colouring

Oven temperature 350°F, 180°C, Gas Mark 4
Grease and line an 8 in (20 cm) round, deep cake tin with greaseproof paper. Grease the paper.

Place the corn oil, sugar, eggs, vanilla essence and ground almonds in a mixing bowl and beat well for 2 to 3 minutes until mixture is smooth and glossy. Peel and finely grate the carrot; peel, core and finely grate the apple. Add the carrot and apple to the bowl with the flour, bicarbonate of soda, baking powder, cinnamon and salt. Mix well. Spoon the mixture into the cake tin. Bake in the centre of the preheated oven for 1 hour 30 minutes to 1 hour 35 minutes.

If cooked, the cake will have begun to shrink from the side of the tin and will spring back if the centre is pressed lightly with the fingertips. Leave the cake in the tin for 5 minutes, then turn out and cool on a wire rack.

To make the frosting: place the cream cheese, butter and vanilla essence in a small bowl and beat well together until soft and creamy. Sieve in the icing sugar and beat well for 1 to 2 minutes until light and fluffy. Spoon onto the cake and spread over the top and side using a palette knife. Mark in swirls.

To make the decoration: divide the marzipan in half. Add a few drops of red and yellow colouring to one half and knead to a deep orange colour. Divide the mixture into eight, shape into carrots and make markings with the back of a knife. Set aside. Colour a tiny piece of remaining almond paste green and use to make carrot fronds and apple leaves. Colour remaining almond paste red and shape into apples, paint on a little green food colouring. Arrange carrots and apples on frosting and attach carrot fronds and apple leaves.

SPICED APPLE AND APRICOT TEA-LOAF

This is a useful recipe if you need to make something for tea but find there are no eggs in the house. It's best kept for a day before eating and will store well for up to 10 days, wrapped in cling film and stored in an airtight tin.

12 oz (375 g) plain flour
pinch of salt
2 tsp (10 ml) baking powder
1 tsp (5 ml) cinnamon
1 tsp (5 ml) nutmeg
6 oz (175 g) butter
2 oz (50 g) chopped walnuts
2 oz (50 g) dried apricots
6 oz (175 g) demerara sugar
4 oz (100 g) sultanas
$\frac{1}{2}$ pt (300 ml) apple purée (made from 1 lb
(450 g) sweet eating apples)
$\frac{1}{4}$ pt (150 ml) milk
1 oz (25 g) demerara sugar, to sprinkle

Oven temperature 350°F, 180°C, Gas Mark 4
Lightly grease and line a 2 lb (900 g) loaf tin with greaseproof paper. Grease the paper.

Sieve the flour, salt, baking powder, cinnamon and nutmeg into a mixing bowl. Add the butter, cut into small pieces and rub in with the fingertips until the mixture resembles fine breadcrumbs. Finely chop the walnuts and apricots. Stir into the mixture with the sugar and sultanas, and mix well. Add the apple purée and the milk, and mix to a soft dropping consistency. Spoon the mixture into the tin and level the top with the back of the spoon.

Bake in the centre of the preheated oven for 1 hour 15 minutes. If cooked, the cake will have begun to shrink from the sides of the tin and the centre will spring back when pressed lightly with fingertips. Leave in the tin for 5 minutes, turn out and cool on a wire rack. Serve plain or well buttered.

APPLE CAKE WITH WALNUTS, ORANGE AND MARZIPAN

This is a moist fruity cake that will keep well for up to 10 days in an airtight tin if you can keep it from the family that long! It also freezes well.

4 oz (100 g) walnut pieces
1 large orange
4 oz (100 g) marzipan
2 sweet eating apples
6 oz (175 g) butter
6 oz (175 g) caster sugar
3 eggs
8 oz (225 g) wholemeal flour
1 tsp (5 ml) baking powder
1 tsp (5 ml) ground cinnamon
3 tblsp (45 ml) milk

Oven temperature 325°F, 170°C, Gas Mark 3
Grease and line an 8 in (20 cm) round, loose-bottomed cake tin with greaseproof paper. Grease the paper.

Coarsely chop the walnut pieces, finely grate the orange rind and squeeze the juice. Cut the marzipan into very small dice. Peel, core and chop the apples.

Beat the butter in a large bowl with the sugar until the mixture is light and creamy. Lightly whisk the eggs and gradually beat into the mixture. Add the flour, baking powder and cinnamon and fold in gently using a metal spoon to make a fairly stiff mixture.

Add the milk, the walnuts, orange rind and juice, marzipan and apple, and stir well until all the ingredients are thoroughly mixed. Spoon the mixture into the prepared tin. Bake in the centre of the preheated oven for 2 hours or until well risen and golden and the cake is beginning to shrink from the sides of the tin.

Allow to sit for 5 minutes then turn out onto a wire cooling tray, remove the greaseproof paper and allow the cake to cool completely.

FIGGY APPLE WHOLEMEAL LOAF

A great cut and come again cake that will keep you going for 10 days! It's made by boiling the ingredients together, so it is speedy to make and quick to mature. Measure the golden syrup carefully making sure you add level spoonfuls.

8 oz (225 g) dried figs
5 oz (150 g) butter
$\frac{1}{4}$ pt (150 ml) milk
6 tblsp (90 ml) golden syrup
4 oz (125 g) plain flour
4 oz (125 g) wholemeal flour
1 tsp (5 ml) ground mixed spice
3 sweet eating apples
2 eggs
$\frac{1}{2}$ tsp (2.5 ml) bicarbonate of soda
2 tblsp (30 ml) demerara sugar

Oven temperature 300°F, 150°C, Gas Mark 2
Grease and line the base of a 2 lb (900 g) loaf tin, with greaseproof paper and grease the paper.

Coarsely chop the figs. Place the butter in a small pan with the milk and syrup and heat gently until the butter melts and the syrup dissolves. Bring to the boil, add the chopped figs and simmer gently for 2 to 3 minutes. Remove the pan from the heat and allow to cool.

Place the plain flour, wholemeal flour and mixed spice into a bowl and mix lightly together. Peel, core and chop two of the apples and lightly whisk the eggs together. Add the cooled milk mixture, the apples, eggs and bicarbonate of soda to the flour mixture and beat well with a wooden spoon until all the ingredients are thoroughly combined. Spoon the mixture into the prepared tin. Peel, core and thinly slice the remaining apple and arrange the slices overlapping on top of the mixture in a line down the centre of the loaf. Sprinkle the top with demerara sugar.

Bake in the centre of the preheated oven for 1 hour 45 minutes to 2 hours or until the cake is well risen and beginning to shrink from the sides of the tin. Allow to cool for 5 minutes then turn out onto a wire cooling rack, remove the paper from the base and allow the cake to cool completely. Cut into thick slices to serve.

DORSET APPLE CAKE

If you ever stop in any tea room in the West Country you will find a cake like this served warm with thick clotted cream. It is moist and crumbly and this particular recipe is quick and simple to make. It is supposed to shrink slightly in the middle.

4 oz (125 g) unsalted butter
4 oz (125 g) light soft brown sugar
1 egg
8 oz (250 g) self-raising flour
1 lb (450 g) cooking apples
2 oz (50 g) sultanas
1 tsp (5 ml) ground ginger
1 tsp (5 ml) ground cinnamon
2 tblsp (30 ml) light soft brown sugar

Oven temperature 350°F, 180°C, Gas Mark 4
Melt the butter in a pan and allow to cool. Add the sugar and the egg and beat well. Stir in the flour and mix well to form a warm, soft dough. Press half of the dough into the base of a 7 in (18 cm) round loose-bottomed cake tin. Peel, core and thinly slice the apples and arrange over the

dough. Scatter the sultanas over and sprinkle well with the ginger, cinnamon and sugar.

Cover with the remaining dough and smooth the top level. Bake in the centre of the preheated oven for 40 to 45 minutes or until golden brown.

WHOLEMEAL CARROT AND APPLE SCONES
makes 8

You'll not use up many apples this way but you will get a moist scone that begs to be buttered and eaten warm.

8 oz (225 g) wholemeal flour
4 tsp (20 ml) baking powder
$\frac{1}{2}$ tsp (2.5 ml) salt
2 oz (50 g) margarine
1 sweet eating apple
1 small carrot
$\frac{1}{4}$ pt (150 ml) milk

Oven temperature 400°F, 200°C, Gas Mark 6
Place the flour, baking powder and salt in a bowl. Add the margarine cut into small pieces and rub in with the fingertips until the mixture resembles breadcrumbs. Peel, core and coarsely grate the apple; scrape and coarsely grate the carrot. Stir in and mix well. Add the milk and mix to a fairly firm dough. Lightly flour the work surface and knead the dough lightly.

Grease a 7 in (18 cm) round sandwich tin and coat with flour. Turn the dough into the tin and knead it lightly to smooth the top. Mark on eight triangles using a sharp knife and cook in the top of the preheated oven for 20 to 25 minutes or until the scone is well risen and golden. Pull apart to serve.

APPLE GINGERBREAD

This is a cake which improves with keeping and should not be eaten the day it is made.

3 oz (75 g) butter
3 oz (75 g) demerara sugar
3 oz (75 g) golden syrup
1 tblsp (15 ml) black treacle
6 oz (175 g) self-raising flour
1 tsp (5 ml) ground mixed spice
1 tsp (5 ml) ground ginger
$\frac{1}{4}$ pt (150 ml) unsweetened apple purée
(made from 1 medium cooking apple)
1 beaten egg

Oven temperature 350°F, 180°C, Gas Mark 4
Butter a large, 9 in by 5 in (23 cm by 12.5 cm) loaf tin. Melt the butter, sugar, syrup and treacle together in a small pan and allow to cool.

Sieve the flour, mixed spice and ginger into a bowl. Beat in the syrup mixture, the apple purée and lastly the beaten egg.

Pour the mixture into the prepared loaf tin and bake in the centre of the preheated oven for approximately 50 minutes or until the gingerbread is beginning to shrink from the sides of the tin. Allow to cool before turning out on to a wire rack.

APPLE SHORTBREAD
makes 8 slices

Shortbread topped with glazed apple slices and chopped nuts is both attractive and delicious.

4 oz (100 g) plain flour
2 oz (50 g) cornflour
2 oz (50 g) caster sugar
4 oz (100 g) softened butter
2 sweet eating apples
1 tblsp (15 ml) melted butter
1 tblsp (15 ml) apple jelly or
sieved apricot jam
1 tblsp (15 ml) chopped almonds

Oven temperature 350°F, 180°C, Gas Mark 4
Sieve the plain flour and cornflour together. Add the sugar and butter and mix well until the mixture forms a firm dough. Lightly butter a shallow 8 in (20 cm) tin and press the dough into the tin.

Bake in the centre of the preheated oven for 20 minutes. Cut the shortbread into 8 slices. Peel, core and thinly slice the apples and arrange them on each slice. Brush the apples with the melted butter and return to the oven for a further 20 minutes.

Melt the jelly or jam, brush over the apple slices and sprinkle with the chopped nuts.

Allow to cool before removing from the tin.

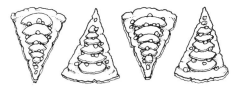

HONEYED APPLE OATMEAL SLICES
makes 8 to 10 slices

These slices, when first baked, are somewhat crumbly and need to be lifted out of the tin very carefully with a palette knife or fish slice to prevent them from breaking. It is worth the effort as they are quite delicious. They seem to improve with keeping.

3 oz (75 g) porridge oats
3 oz (75 g) wholemeal flour
1½ oz (40 g) soft brown sugar
6 oz (175 g) butter

Topping
6 oz (175 g) cooking apples
1½ oz (40 g) butter
3 tblsp (45 ml) clear honey

Oven temperature 350°F, 180°C, Gas Mark 4
Mix the porridge oats, flour and sugar together in a bowl. Melt the butter and stir it into the oat mixture. Press the mixture into a shallow buttered cake tin 7 in by 11 in (18 cm by 28 cm).

Peel, core and chop the apples and spread carefully over the base. Melt together the butter and honey and pour over the apples taking care that it does not quite reach the edges. Cover with foil and bake in the centre of the preheated oven for 30 minutes. Remove the foil and bake a further 15 minutes. Cool in the tin before cutting.

PRESERVES

APPLE JELLY

Apple jelly is one of the most useful preserves to keep in the store cupboard. It is an excellent filling for cakes and makes a superb glaze for open tarts. It can be flavoured with other fruits; cranberries and elderberries produce a deep colour and rich flavour. Herbs can be added to make a savoury jelly to accompany cold meat: mint, thyme or rosemary with lamb, sage with pork — the combinations are as various as the herbs themselves.

If you have the apples, any variety can be used but cooking apples such as Bramleys produce the most juice. It is well worth making several batches, some plain and some flavoured.

You will need a large preserving pan, a jelly bag and somewhere out of the way to hang the bag, preferably overnight, whilst the juice drips through.

MASTER RECIPE

Wash the fruit and cut out any bruises. Cut the apples into quarters but do not peel or core and place them in a preserving pan with $\frac{1}{2}$ pt (300 ml) of water to each 1 lb (450 g) of apple. Bring to simmering point and cook, stirring occasionally, until the fruit is soft and pulpy.

Place a jelly bag inside a large bowl and ladle the cooked apples and their juice into it. Tie the bag firmly and hang it somewhere safe. Leave it to drip overnight. Resist the temptation to squeeze it or the jelly will not be clear.

Measure the juice back into the preserving pan and for every 1 pt (600 ml) of juice add 1 lb (450 g) of sugar. Heat gently until all the sugar has dissolved. Then bring it rapidly to the boil, without stirring, until it reaches setting point.

A considerable amount of foamy scum will rise to the surface whilst the jelly boils. Leave it until setting point and remove it in one go. Pour into warm jars, cover and seal.

(The strained pulp left in the jelly bag can be used to make a very stiff purée. As it contains all the pips and skins it needs to be sieved — hard work as it is far stiffer than ordinary purée!)

ELDERBERRY AND APPLE JELLY

Follow the master recipe for apple jelly but just before bottling trail a sprig of fresh elderberries through the jelly. The colour and flavour will run immediately. Stir lightly to mix. Bottle and seal.

CRANBERRY AND APPLE JELLY

Follow the master recipe for apple jelly but add 2 oz (50 g) of cranberries to each 1 pt (600 ml) of apple juice.

BLACKBERRY AND APPLE JELLY

Follow the master recipe for apple jelly but use half blackberries and half apples.

HERB JELLIES

No jelly will keep well for long once it is opened and, as herb jellies are eaten less frequently than ordinary jams, it is best to bottle it in small jars. If you are using a variety of herbs boil the juice and sugar in small quantities so that each batch can be flavoured separately.

Follow the master recipe for apple jelly. When it reaches setting point remove the scum and add fresh chopped herbs (dried if fresh are not available). The amount of herbs can be as much or as little as you like but 2 to 3 tblsp (30 to 45 ml) to each 1 lb (450 g) of jelly is a good guide. Leave to cool for a minute or two then stir to distribute the herbs. Bottle and seal.

AUTUMN JAM
makes around 6 lb (2.7 kg) jam

An excellent way of using up mixed windfalls but so good that it is worth buying the extra fruit if you do not have your own.

$1\frac{1}{2}$ lb (675 g) plums
$1\frac{1}{2}$ lb (675 g) cooking apples
1 lb (450 g) pears
3 lb (1.4 kg) sugar
knob of butter

Halve the plums and remove the stones. Place the plum stones in a pan with $\frac{1}{2}$ pt (300 ml) of water. Peel, core and chop the apples and pears into large pieces. Add the cores and peelings to the plum stones and boil for about 20 minutes.

Mix the plums, apples and pears in a preserving pan. Strain in the water from the stones and skins and bring to the boil. Simmer until the fruit is tender, stirring from time to time so that it does not stick to the bottom. (The time will depend on the variety and ripeness of the fruit.)

Stir in the sugar and heat slowly until it dissolves, then boil rapidly stirring until the jam has set.

Remove from the heat, stir in the knob of butter to clear the scum from the top of the jam.

Pour into warm jam jars, cover, cool and label.

APPLE LEMON PRESERVE
makes around 3 lb (1.4 kg)

A light and delicate preserve which should not be allowed to set too hard.

2 lb (900 g) cooking apples
2 medium-sized lemons
1½lb (675 g) sugar

Peel, core and slice the apples into a heavy pan. Add enough water to cover the apples — approximately 2 pt (1.1 l); cover and simmer until the apples are completely soft. Sieve and return them to the pan.

Squeeze the juice from the lemons and add with the sugar. Cook over a low heat to dissolve the sugar, then boil rapidly until setting point is just reached.

Pour into warm jam jars, cover, cool and label.

APPLE AND LEMON CURD
makes 3 lb (1.4 kg)

A welcome change to keep in the store cupboard but one which does not keep too long — about 2 months in a cold place — so it is unwise to make it in large quantities.

2 lb (900 g) cooking apples
8 oz (225 g) sugar
8 oz (225 g) butter
2 eggs
juice of 1 medium-sized lemon

Peel, core and slice the apples into a pan. Simmer them with a little water until soft. Sieve and return to the pan.

Add the sugar and butter and beat well until the butter has melted and the sugar dissolved. Beat the eggs thoroughly and add to the apple mixture. Stirring constantly, cook over a very gentle heat until it has thickened. Stir in the lemon juice.

Pour into warm jam jars, cover, cool and label.

ORCHARD CHUTNEY
makes 3 lb (1.4 kg)

A light, fresh-tasting chutney that is particularly good with cold roast pork. Sharp and fruity.

1 lb (450 g) cooking apples
1 lb (450 g) pears
8 oz (225 g) onions
1 medium-sized lemon
$\frac{1}{2}$ pt (300 ml) vinegar
$\frac{1}{4}$ tsp (1.25 ml) ground cinnamon
$\frac{1}{4}$ tsp (1.25 ml) ground ginger
pinch ground cloves
8 oz (225 g) light brown sugar

Peel, core and chop the apples and pears; peel and chop the onions. Finely grate the rind of the lemon and squeeze the juice. Add the lemon rind to the pan with the vinegar, cinnamon, ginger and cloves and simmer until the apples and pears are tender. Add the sugar and lemon juice and cook slowly over a low heat to dissolve the sugar, then boil rapidly until thick. Pour into warm jam jars, cover, cool and label.

MANDARIN AND APPLE CHUTNEY
makes 4 lb (1.8 kg)

This thick, dark chutney is best made as soon as the mandarin oranges appear in the shops early in October. Then it will have plenty of time to mature, ready for serving with Christmas hams.

8 oz (225 g) seedless mandarin oranges
1 lb (450 g) ripe tomatoes
1 lb (450 g) cooking apples
1 lb (450 g) large onions
3 cloves of garlic
8 oz (225 g) stoned dates
2 tsp (10 ml) salt
1 tblsp (15 ml) ground cloves
1 tblsp (15 ml) ground coriander
2 pts (1.1 l) malt vinegar
2 lb (900 g) soft dark brown sugar
4 oz (125 g) black treacle

Finely chop the mandarin oranges, including the skin, or run briefly through a food processor. Skin the tomatoes and chop roughly. Peel, core and chop the apples, peel and chop the onions and garlic, and coarsely chop the dates.

Place the mandarin oranges, tomatoes, apple, onion, garlic and dates in a large pan with the salt, cloves, coriander and 1 pt (550 ml) of the vinegar. Bring to the boil, reduce the heat and simmer for 1 hour 30 minutes stirring occasionally until the mixture is soft and pulpy.

Add the remaining 1 pt vinegar, the sugar and treacle and simmer for a further 15 minutes until the mixture has thickened. Ladle the chutney into warmed jars; cover while still hot. Store for 2 or 3 months before using.

TOMATO AND APPLE CHUTNEY
makes 3 lb (1.4 kg)

Tomatoes and apples make good partners for this mild, velvety chutney. Good with salt beef, salami, strong cheese or an accompaniment to curry.

2 lb (900 g) ripe tomatoes
1½ lb (675 g) cooking apples
8 oz (225 g) onions
1 tblsp (15 ml) paprika
¼ tsp (1.25 ml) cinnamon
¼ tsp (1.25 ml) cayenne pepper
2 tsp (10 ml) salt
8 oz (225 g) granulated sugar
¼ pt (150 ml) malt vinegar

Skin the tomatoes, cut them in quarters and place in a preserving pan. Peel, core and chop the apples, peel and chop the onions, and add them to the tomatoes with the paprika, cinnamon, cayenne pepper and salt. Cook over a low heat, stirring occasionally until the mixture has reduced by about half and is thick and pulpy.

Add the sugar and vinegar, heat gently, stirring until the sugar has dissolved, and boil until the chutney is thick. Pour into warm jam jars, cover, cool and label.

APPLE, MARROW AND GINGER CHUTNEY
makes 3 lb (1.4 kg)

A good way to use up marrows to make a spicy chutney.

1 lb (450 g) marrow, weighed when
peeled and cored
1 oz (25 g) salt
1 lb (450 g) onions
2 lb (900 g) cooking apples
$\frac{1}{2}$ oz (15 g) root ginger
$\frac{1}{2}$ oz (15 g) chilli peppers
$\frac{1}{2}$ oz (15 g) black peppercorns
$\frac{1}{2}$ pt (300 ml) malt vinegar
8 oz (225 g) sugar

Cut the marrow flesh into small cubes, sprinkle on the salt and leave to drain in a colander overnight, or for several hours.

Peel and chop the onions, peel, core and chop the apples. Beat the ginger with a rolling pin to crush. Tie the ginger, chilli peppers and peppercorns in a piece of muslin and simmer with the marrow, onions and apples until the onion is tender. Add the vinegar and sugar and boil, stirring frequently to prevent them sticking to the bottom of the pan, until the chutney is thick. Remove the bag of spices. Pour into warm jam jars, cover, cool and label.

APPLE AND GREEN TOMATO CHUTNEY
makes around 4 lb (1.7 kg)

Green tomatoes give quite a different flavour to chutney from ripened ones. This is a full-bodied chutney that is excellent with cold roast pork.

2 lb (900 g) cooking apples
1 lb (450 g) onions
1½ lb (675 g) green tomatoes
¾ pt (450 ml) malt vinegar
12 oz (350 g) dark brown sugar
1 tsp (5 ml) ground ginger
½ tsp (2.5 ml) cinnamon
1 tsp (5 ml) salt

Peel, core and slice the apples; peel and slice the onions and slice the tomatoes. Place the apples, onions and tomatoes in a preserving pan, add the vinegar, sugar, ginger, cinnamon and salt and cook over a medium heat, stirring frequently, until the chutney has thickened.

Pour into warm jam jars, cover, cool and label.

UNCOOKED APPLE AND BANANA CHUTNEY
makes about 5 lbs (2.3 kg)

This is a useful recipe that can be made all the year round. It keeps well for up to 1 year and is good served with mild cheeses and cold meat.

3 medium bananas
1 lb (450 g) onions
1 lb (450 g) cooking apples
1 lb (450 g) sultanas
8 oz (225 g) currants
1 lb (450 g) demerara sugar
$\frac{1}{2}$ pt (300 ml) dark malt vinegar
1 tsp (5 ml) salt
$\frac{1}{2}$ tsp (2.5 ml) cayenne pepper

Peel and mash the bananas; peel and roughly chop the onions. Peel, core and roughly chop the apples; chop the sultanas and currants. Place the bananas, onions, apples, sultanas and currants in a large bowl with the sugar, vinegar, salt and cayenne and mix well. Pot, seal and label.

APPLE, DATE AND WALNUT MINCEMEAT
makes about 5 lb (2.3 kg)

Apple keeps mincemeat moist and adds a tartness. This recipe will keep well for up to 1 year and is best made a couple of months before Christmas to allow it to mature.

1 small carrot
1 large cooking apple
8 oz (225 g) stoned dates
8 oz (225 g) sultanas
4 oz (125 g) dried apricots
4 oz (125 g) glacé cherries
6 oz (175 g) shelled walnut pieces
4 oz (125 g) raisins
8 oz (225 g) shredded suet
10 oz (275 g) golden demerara sugar
1 tsp (5 ml) ground cinnamon
1 tsp (5 ml) ground nutmeg
1 tsp (5 ml) ground cloves
1 tsp (5 ml) ground coriander
3 tangerine oranges
$\frac{1}{4}$ pt (150 ml) dark rum or whisky

Peel and coarsely grate the carrot; peel, core and coarsely chop the apple; finely chop the dates, sultanas, apricots, cherries and walnuts. Place the carrot, apple, dates, sultanas, apricots, cherries and walnuts in a large bowl with the raisins, suet, sugar, cinnamon, nutmeg, cloves and coriander. Finely grate the rind of the tangerines and squeeze the juice. Add to the fruit mixture with the rum or whisky and stir well to mix. Cover and leave for 2 days, stirring occasionally. Pot, seal and label.

THE
ALCOHOLIC
APPLE

One way of cutting down on the booze bill is to make your own wine and cider. Apples make some of the very best country wines, which can be made in small quantities with the minimum of equipment. The crushed apples are diluted with water and fermented; the better the quality of the fruit the better the results, but windfalls can be used as long as all the bruised bits are cut out.

It is a more exacting process than making cider, which is quite simply fermented apple juice. Wine takes longer to ferment and actually improves with age whereas cider can be drunk within a few months and is at its best when still young.

For cider the apples need not, indeed should not, be in perfect condition provided they are not actually black, and it is the perfect way of putting a large quantity of windfalls to good use. However, cider is a drink to be quaffed rather than sipped and not really worth making in less than 5 gallon (23 l) quantities. One solitary gallon will disappear before you know it. So if your apples can be measured in pounds rather than hundredweights stick to apple wine and treasure it.

Apple Wine

If you are going to go through the agonising but worth-while wait for your apples to become a delicious alcoholic liquid then it is worth taking a bit of trouble over the initial preparation.

Remove the stalks from the apples and wash them thoroughly in cold running water, scrubbing the skins with a nail brush to remove any invisible bugs that might lurk on the surface. Crush or cut them into small pieces — there is no need to peel or core them. Power-driven crushers that you attach to an electric drill make life easy but you can use a food processor, a mincer, a liquidiser or, at worst, do it by hand.

If you don't have time to make wine at harvest time and you have plenty of freezer space, cut the apples up and to prevent them going brown drop them into a solution of 1 crushed campden tablet to 1 gallon (5.1 l) of water and stir well to mix. Drain and weigh the apples, label and freeze. Leave the apples in the sealed bags until they have thawed and follow the recipe for using fresh apples.

As a final note, do keep a record of the apples you used as there is nothing more frustrating than producing a really excellent wine and not being able to remember which apples you used to make it.

DRY APPLE WINE
makes 6 bottles

4½ pt (2.5 l) cold water
1 tsp (5 ml) citric acid
½ tsp (2.5 ml) tannin
approx 2 tsp (10 ml) pectin enzyme (or as
directed on pack)
2 campden tablets
9 lb (4 kg) mixed cooking apples
yeast nutrient (as directed on pack)
champagne yeast
½ pt (300 ml) white grape juice concentrate
1¾ lb (800 g) granulated sugar

Measure the water into a large plastic bucket, add the citric acid, the tannin, the pectin enzyme and 1 campden tablet crushed between two spoons. Stir with a wooden spoon to mix.

Wash and crush the apples and add immediately to the water, cover and leave in a warm place for 24 hours. This breaks down the natural pectin which will give you more juice and a clearer wine. At the same time add a little yeast nutrient to the yeast, with about ¼ pt (150 ml) warm boiled water. Pour into a sterilised wine bottle, bung the top with cotton wool and leave in a warm place for 24 hours, shaking the bottle occasionally.

The next day stir the activated yeast and the grape juice concentrate into the apple mixture. Cover the apples with a large clean plate to keep the apples submerged, cover the bin and leave in a warm place for 7 days, stirring twice a day.

Strain the fruit through a fruit press, a jelly bag or a clean tea towel suspended over a plastic colander, pressing the fruit well until it is quite dry and all the juice has been extracted. Stir the sugar into the strained liquid, pour it into a sterilised demijohn and top up with cold, boiled water if necessary to bring the level to within 1 in (2.5 cm) of the neck of the jar. Label the wine, fit an airlock and store the demijohn in a warm place until bubbles no longer pass through the airlock and the wine begins to clear.

Siphon the wine into another sterilised demijohn, leaving the sediment at the bottom, top up with cold boiled water and add a crushed campden tablet. Fit a solid bung to the top of the jar and store in a cool place for 3 months.

After 3 months the wine should be clear. If it is still cloudy add finings according to the instructions on the pack and leave for 1 week. Siphon the wine into another sterilised jar and store for a further 6 months in a cool place.

Siphon the wine into clean sterilised bottles, cork, label and store in a cool place for 3 months before drinking.

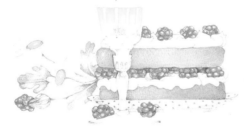

Sparkling Wine

The wine can be turned very successfully into a crisp sparkling wine at the bottling stage. Use only champagne or sparkling wine bottles because they're specially strengthened to withstand the extra pressure of the gas produced by fermenting the wine in the bottle. Your local hotel can probably supply you with some and make sure they are free from chips and scratches which might weaken them.

Add $2\frac{1}{2}$ oz (70 g) of caster sugar to the wine when it is ready for bottling and mix a champagne yeast with a little yeast nutrient and water to get it started. Add the yeast to the liquid, fit an airlock and leave in a warm place for a few hours until fermentation starts. Siphon the slightly fermenting wine into sterilised champagne bottles to within 2 in (5 cm) of the top. Fit with sterilised hollow plastic stoppers, cover with wire cages and twist with a pair of pliers to fasten. Label the bottles and store on their sides in a warm place for at least 6 months, preferably a year.

After this time you will see sediment lying down the edge of the bottle. Place the bottles, neck down, in a cardboard bottle box, at an angle of 45° and twist the bottles every day for about 4 weeks to slide the sediment into the hollow in the stopper. Stand the bottles completely upside down in the box for a few days. Stand each bottle in a jug of crushed ice for about 10 minutes so that the sediment in the neck of the bottle is frozen. Carefully remove the stopper and place your thumb over the neck to stop the wine pouring out. Quickly replace the stopper with a sterilised one and replace the wire cage. Chill the wine on its side before opening.

Cider

Few people have their own 'cider' apples which give cider its characteristic flavour but ordinary apples can be used to make an excellent brew which tastes better than many commercially made ciders. Well-flavoured apples are essential for a good cider but dessert apples on their own are seldom sufficiently acid and should be mixed with cooking apples. We are reliably informed that crab apples or pears will also increase the astringency. Some people consider Bramleys too acid but we have found that they make a very quaffable cider.

For home-made cider you will need a good supply of apples, some means of crushing and pressing them, suitable non-metal containers for fermenting plus the winemaker's paraphernalia of bungs, airlocks and siphoning tubes. You should also plan in advance somewhere to dump the remains of the pressed apples as they take a long time to rot down. If you are making a large amount of cider it is well worthwhile contacting a farmer who could feed them to his animals. Pigs seem to thrive on the stuff, but you must get it to them fast, before it starts fermenting, as a drunk pig is not a pretty sight!

The power-driven crushers which attach to an electric drill can be used in conjunction with the small fruit presses which can be bought at most wine-making shops. But if you have several mature trees and plan to make a year's supply of cider you will certainly need a good sized crusher and press. It is not cheap but it does pay for itself very quickly, quicker still if you share the equipment with neighbours.

A considerable economy can be made if you are able to make the equipment yourself. The crusher we use is little more than an outsized rolling pin studded with stainless steel screws and powered by the motor from an old washing machine. A medium-sized press can be constructed on the same lines as an old-fashioned screw press. The one illustrated is a small scale version of the press we use, but the necessary pressure is produced by a hydraulic car jack.

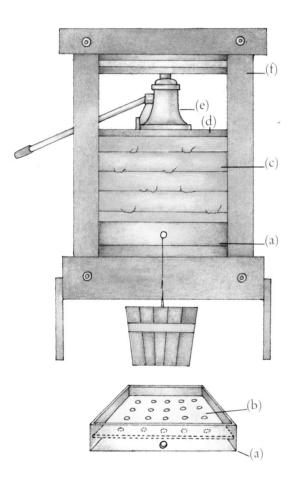

The box (a) *has a perforated tray* (b) *inside to allow the juice to flow through.*

The cheeses (c), *crushed apples wrapped in hessian squares, using a box the same size as* (a) *as a mould, are pressed between the tray and the pressure board* (d) *by the jack* (e).

As the jack expands further 'distance boards' (f) *are inserted at the top.*

Making Cider

Crush the apples first, then extract as much juice as possible by passing them through a press. You will need to wear rubber gloves when handling crushed apples to prevent your hands being stained brown. Strain the apple juice into sterilised fermenting vessels, fill them right up to the top and keep a little juice aside for topping up. Do not bung but cover the opening with an upturned cup.

Traditionally, cider is fermented with no extra sugar or yeast. It is, however, a wise precaution to add extra yeast in cold weather, but only wine yeast should be added, not baker's or brewer's. Some people add sugar, but this is a matter of taste; we do find that the very acid apples are improved by adding around 8 oz (225 g) sugar to a gallon of juice.

For the first few days the fermentation is very vigorous; a thick froth appears which must be allowed to spill out as it contains impurities. Keep the fermenting liquid topped right up and once it has settled down fit a bung and airlock.

An easy-to-make apple crusher

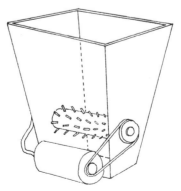

The cider will be very cloudy at first but will gradually clear. Once it has cleared and only a few bubbles rise to the surface, siphon it into another fermenting vessel and fit a clean airlock. Leave it for a few weeks, tasting from time to time. If it tastes over-sweet leave it to ferment a little longer. When you are happy with the taste siphon some of the cider into bottles for immediate use. We find with a large quantity that it is too much of a chore to bottle it all individually so we siphon it into the large plastic containers used for sherry. These are useful as they have a tap on the side for drawing off the cider.

(They can also be used for fermenting cider in if they are placed on their side with the tap on top. A piece of flexible pipe can be fitted on the top and trailed into a jar of water making a very simple but effective airlock.)

One last word of warning. Do not be in too much of a hurry to bottle your cider. If you do you may end up with what Sir Paul Neil so charmingly described in his *Discourse of Cider* as 'that sort which some people call Potgun-drink that when you open the bottles it will fly about the house and be so windy and cutting that it will be inconvenient to drink'!

Cider Vinegar

Cider converts easily to cider vinegar and the most reliable way is to mix 5 parts of cider to 1 part of bought cider vinegar. Half-fill a demijohn and plug the top loosely with cotton wool and store in a warm place WELL AWAY FROM ANY FERMENTING WINE OR CIDER. The vinegar will become cloudy at first and form a skin on the top. Leave for about 8 weeks and siphon into bottles. (KEEP THE SIPHON STRICTLY FOR VINEGAR ONLY.)

Apple Juice

Domestic juice extractors or the fruit presses can be used to make apple juice. It does not keep well, unless it is properly pasteurised, so we recommend you make it fresh or make it in large quantities, freeze it in small cartons and defrost it as required.

Equipment for Wine and Cider Making

Basic equipment is available from wine-making shops and most branches of Boots the Chemists. Two firms who specialise in large size crushers and presses, which come complete with instructions, are:

Loftus Mail Order
9 Oakleigh Way
Mitcham
Surrey
CR4 1AU

Vineyard & Grower Supplies
Great Job's Cross Farm
The Oast House
Wassall Lane, Cnr (A28)
Rolvenden, Kent

APPLES FOR THE GARDEN

An enormous range of apple varieties is available to the home grower and, with careful planning and enough storage space, you can eat your own apples from summer to spring. You do not need a huge garden to grow several varieties, because apple trees can be quite small. The ultimate size an apple tree reaches is determined by the root-stock on which it is grown. Sizes vary from tiny 'bondsais' to full-size trees. Here are some points to consider when selecting varieties:

- Decide what size is most suitable. Small trees fruit sooner and are easier to manage.
- Select varieties which ripen at different times for a succession of apples.
- For successful pollination (necessary for trees to bear fruit) select varieties which flower at the same time; two or more from each flowering period unless one is a triploid, when you will need three.
- It is better in the long run to buy young trees grown in open ground, even if they look disappointingly small, than large pot-grown trees. You will get fruit just as soon and will get a better shaped tree provided you prune correctly.

The subject of pruning is beyond the scope of this book: it is explained in detail in the many books on fruit growing. Methods vary according to the shape of the tree, so read how to do it before you get out the secateurs!

It is not always easy to find good nurseries, but most countries have apple advisory services which can help. In Britain the following nurseries have a good selection:

Allgroves Nurseries
Middle Green
Langley
Bucks

Enormous selection of old
and new varieties includes a
few cider apples. Rather
limited choice of root-stocks.

Michael Cook
Keepers Nursery
446 Waterinbury Road
East Malling
Kent

Good selection of old,
new and cider varieties. Will
also propagate almost any
variety to order.

Deacons Nursery
Godshill
Isle of Wight

Large choice of old and new
varieties plus small selection
of cider apples.

Highfield Nurseries
Whitminster
Gloucester

Small but good selection
includes many new varieties.

R V Rogers Ltd
The Nurseries
Pickering
North Yorkshire

Smaller selection, not many
new varieties but all are
suitable for growing in
the North.

Scotts Nurseries
Merriott
Somerset

Large selection includes
old and unusual varieties.

INDEX